OCCUPATIONAL PSYCHOSIS

OCCUPATIONAL PSYCHOSIS

Volume II
Institutional Failure Modes

GEORGIA LEE ARTS

Founder and Director
Occupational Wellness Institute™

Copyright and Publication Notice

Occupational Psychosis: Volume II, Institutional Failure Modes

"*Occupational Psychosis*" is a conceptual and structural term used for analytic purposes. It is not a clinical diagnosis and does not refer to psychiatric classification or individual mental health conditions.

This volume forms part of the Occupational Psychosis canon.

This volume is analytic in nature. It does not establish governance standards, confer certification authority, or provide operational assessment frameworks. Matters of implementation, measurement methodology, certification, and professional application are stewarded separately.

Published by the Occupational Wellness Institute™
Menomonie, WI

https://occupationalwellnessinstitute.org

ISBN: 979-8-9941272-0-9 (hardcover)

Printed in the United States of America

CANON DESIGNATION

This volume forms part of the *Occupational Psychosis* canon, a structured body of work examining role-induced distortion within authority systems.

The canon is organized as a sequential and integrated series:

- Volume I – *The Hidden Crisis Beneath Occupational Wellness*
- Volume II – *Institutional Failure Modes*
- Volume III – *Authority, Ethics, and Governance (Institutional)*

Subsequent volumes extend the canon across stewardship, professional boundaries, and long-term institutional design. Each volume serves a distinct analytic or institutional function.

This volume is limited to structural classification and systemic analysis.

PUBLISHER'S NOTE

Occupational Psychosis, Volume II - Institutional Failure Modes extends the definitional foundation established in Volume I by examining the structural conditions under which role-induced distortion may manifest within authority systems.

This volume does not evaluate specific organizations, professions, or sectors. Its analysis remains systemic rather than individual. The focus is on recurring structural patterns that emerge where occupational identity, authority structures, incentive systems, and institutional narratives intersect in ways that constrain reflexivity and normalize deviation over time.

The purpose of this work is analytic and classificatory. It names and organizes institutional failure modes in order to strengthen conceptual clarity within the emerging field of Occupational Psychosis. It does not prescribe reform, establish governance standards, or provide operational assessment frameworks. Matters of implementation, formal measurement methodology, certification, and professional application are stewarded separately within the broader canon and under the institutional auspices of the Occupational Wellness Institute™.

By maintaining analytic restraint, this volume contributes to disciplined inquiry rather than institutional critique. Its function is to clarify structural probabilities and recurring dynamics so that future governance, authority, and stewardship discussions may proceed on a stable conceptual foundation.

SCOPE STATEMENT AND CANON PLACEMENT

This volume examines institutional and occupational failure modes associated with Occupational Psychosis. It proceeds from the definitional foundation established in Volume I and shifts the focus from conceptual clarification to structural manifestation.

The purpose of this volume is analytic and classificatory. It identifies recurring structural conditions, drift patterns, and observable indicators that increase the probability of role-induced distortion within authority systems. The analysis remains systemic in orientation and does not attribute dysfunction to individual character, profession, or sector. Rather, it examines how identity-role fusion, authority insulation, incentive alignment, and narrative reinforcement may converge in ways that impair reflexivity and normalize deviation over time.

This volume does not prescribe reform, establish governance standards, confer certification authority, or present operational implementation frameworks. It does not provide diagnostic instruments, scoring methodologies, or applied assessment tools. The indicators described herein are conceptual and descriptive, intended to advance field literacy and structural understanding.

Matters of governance, corrective architecture, operational measurement, and professional application are governed separately within the Occupational Psychosis canon and, where applicable, under the stewardship of the Occupational Wellness Institute™.

The function of this volume is therefore limited and precise: to name, classify, and clarify institutional failure patterns without directing intervention. In doing so, it strengthens the conceptual infrastructure necessary for responsible authority and future governance development while maintaining analytic restraint.

METHODOLOGICAL ORIENTATION

This volume proceeds through structural and interdisciplinary analysis rather than empirical case study or sector-specific investigation. Its purpose is conceptual clarification and pattern classification.

The analysis draws upon established domains of scholarship including organizational theory, institutional sociology, systems theory, authority studies, professional ethics, and governance research. These disciplines collectively examine how authority structures function, how incentives shape behavior, how narratives influence institutional legitimacy, and how feedback mechanisms sustain or constrain corrective action. The framework developed in this volume synthesizes these traditions to identify recurring structural conditions associated with institutional distortion.

The approach is probabilistic rather than accusatory. It does not assert that institutions are inherently dysfunctional, nor that authority inevitably produces corruption. Rather, it identifies structural configurations that increase the likelihood of reflexive collapse when corrective mechanisms weaken or when role identity becomes fused with institutional legitimacy.

No single data set or sector is under evaluation. The taxonomy presented herein is classificatory, constructed through comparative structural reasoning across domains of authority. Its purpose is to clarify conceptual relationships, not to render empirical judgment about specific organizations or professional communities.

This volume remains intentionally non-instrumental. While the patterns described may be observable and measurable under appropriate methodological conditions, operational assessment frameworks, scoring models, and applied diagnostic tools are not included here. Such methodologies require governance oversight and professional boundary conditions beyond the scope of this volume.

The analytic posture is therefore limited and disciplined: to name structural dynamics, organize failure modes, and clarify the conditions under which institutional distortion becomes more probable. Questions of governance, corrective architecture, and formal measurement are addressed separately within the broader Occupational Psychosis canon.

TERMINOLOGY CLARIFICATION

The term *psychosis* in this volume is used conceptually and structurally rather than clinically. It does not refer to psychiatric diagnosis, individual mental illness, or DSM-classified conditions. No implication is made regarding the mental health status of individuals, professionals, or institutional actors.

Within the framework of Occupational Psychosis, the term functions as an analytic metaphor to describe systemic distortion in perception, reflexivity, and feedback processing that may arise within authority structures under certain structural conditions. The focus is institutional rather than individual.

The framework does not pathologize professions, organizations, or sectors. Nor does it suggest that institutional dysfunction is inevitable. Rather, it identifies configurations in which occupational identity, authority insulation, incentive alignment, and narrative reinforcement may converge in ways that constrain corrective signals and normalize deviation over time.

The use of the term reflects a structural analogy. As clinical psychosis involves impaired reality-testing at the individual level, occupational psychosis describes impaired institutional reality-testing at the systemic level. The analogy is descriptive and bounded. It is not diagnostic, medical, or psychiatric in application.

Readers are therefore encouraged to interpret the terminology within its defined conceptual scope. The framework advances structural analysis of authority systems and should not be construed as commentary on individual psychological conditions.

STATEMENT OF ANALYTIC RESTRAINT

This volume is limited to structural analysis and classification. It does not evaluate specific organizations, professions, or sectors, nor does it render judgment regarding institutional intent or moral character. The patterns described herein represent structural probabilities rather than determinations of fault.

The purpose of this work is to clarify recurring configurations that may increase the likelihood of role-induced distortion within authority systems. It does not authorize reform initiatives, prescribe corrective interventions, or establish governance standards. Such matters require defined authority structures, professional boundaries, and methodological safeguards beyond the scope of this volume.

Readers are therefore advised to interpret the taxonomy and indicators presented here as conceptual tools for disciplined inquiry rather than instruments for immediate application. Responsible implementation, where appropriate, requires governance oversight and formal methodological design.

This restraint is intentional. The stability of an emerging field depends not only on what is named, but on how and when application occurs.

CONTENT

Publisher's Note vi
Scope Statement and Canon Placement vii
Methodological Orientation viii
Terminology Clarification x
Statement of Analytic Restraint xi

PART I. STRUCTURAL PRECONDITIONS

1. From Definition to Manifestation 19
2. Identity–Role Fusion and Occupational Enclosure 25
3. Authority Insulation and Reflexive Collapse 29
4. Metric Substitution and Performance Substitution 33
5. Incentive Alignment and Moral Drift 37
6. Narrative Capture and Legitimacy Protection 41

PART II. INSTITUTIONAL FAILURE MODES

7. Epistemic Narrowing 47
8. Feedback Suppression 51
9. Incentivized Conformity 55
10. Symbolic Compliance 59
11. Authority Inflation 63
12. Moral Credentialing 67
13. Care-Language Shielding 71
14. Crisis Normalization 75
15. Boundary Erosion 79

PART III. SYSTEMIC DRIFT DYNAMICS

16. Gradualism and Normalization of Deviation 85
17. Diffusion of Responsibility 89
18. Reputation Preservation Cycles 93
19. Professional Identity Lock-In 97
20. Self-Reinforcing Authority Loops 103

PART IV. EARLY WARNING INDICATORS

21. Signal Attenuation Across Hierarchical Layers 109
22. Recalibration Delay Under Non-Crisis Conditions 113
23. Narrative Over-Integration of Corrective Feedback 117
24. Metric Stability Amid Outcome Variance 121
25. Interpretive Convergence Without Contestability 125
26. Adaptive Language Without Structural Shift 129

PART V. LIMITS OF DETECTION

27. Why Institutional Actors Rarely Perceive Distortion 135
28. Structural Barriers to Internal Correction 139
29. External Barriers to Accountability 143
30. When Correction Becomes Structurally Impossible 149
31. The Epistemic Boundary of Institutional Analysis 155

ANALYTIC BOUNDARIES (Concluding Section)

32. What This Volume Does Not Do 161
33. Distinction from Governance and Reform 165
34. Conditions for Responsible Application 169

CONCLUSION:
From Failure Modes to Institutional Responsibility 172

Glossary of Structural Terms 173
References 179
Citation Guidance 195
Canon Index 197
About the Author 199
Index 200

"Purposive action may have consequences which are unintended and unrecognized."

- Robert K. Merton

PART I

STRUCTURAL PRECONDITIONS

INTRODUCTION:
STRUCTURAL PRECONDITIONS

Volume I defined *Occupational Psychosis* as a structural phenomenon characterized by impaired institutional reality-testing under specific configurations of identity, authority, incentive, and narrative reinforcement. That volume clarified the conceptual boundaries of the phenomenon without examining how such configurations emerge within functioning authority systems. Part I turns to those conditions.

Institutions depend on specialization, hierarchy, professional identity, and coordinated narrative coherence to function at scale. These features are not inherently distortive; they enable continuity, accountability, and mission alignment. However, when certain structural variables align without countervailing corrective mechanisms, reflexive capacity may narrow.

The chapters that follow examine these variables individually. Each represents a structural condition that, in isolation, may be benign or functionally necessary. It is their interaction and reinforcement over time that increases vulnerability to distortion.

The purpose of Part I is analytic clarification. Before institutional failure modes can be systematically classified, the structural conditions that make their emergence more probable must be understood.

CHAPTER 1

FROM DEFINITION TO MANIFESTATION

Volume I established Occupational Psychosis as a structural phenomenon rather than a clinical condition. It defined the term as role-induced distortion that may arise when occupational identity, authority structures, incentive systems, and institutional narratives converge in ways that impair reflexivity and weaken corrective feedback. Volume I focused on conceptual clarification and defined the phenomenon without attributing pathology to individuals or professions.

This volume proceeds from that definitional foundation and turns to manifestation. The analytic question is no longer what Occupational Psychosis is, but under what structural conditions it becomes more probable.

Institutions depend on specialization, authority delegation, professional identity, and narrative coherence in order to function. These elements enable coordination, continuity, and scale. They allow complex systems to organize knowledge, distribute responsibility, and maintain operational stability over time.

The same structural features that permit institutional effectiveness can, under certain configurations, constrain reflexive correction. The movement from definition to manifestation therefore requires a shift in the analytic focus, from conceptual architecture to systemic configuration.

Occupational Psychosis does not emerge from singular decisions or isolated leadership failures. It becomes more likely when multiple structural conditions align.

First, occupational identity may become fused with institutional legitimacy. When professional self-concept is deeply intertwined with the moral narrative of the organization, critique can be experienced not as procedural correction but as existential threat. Under such conditions, the capacity to differentiate role from identity narrows.

Second, authority insulation may reduce exposure to disconfirming feedback. Hierarchical distance, credential barriers, and reputational incentives can collectively weaken channels through which corrective signals travel. Over time, insulation may produce informational asymmetry between leadership levels and operational realities.

Third, incentive systems may reward conformity more consistently than correction. When advancement, funding, or professional recognition depends upon maintaining narrative stability, the cost of dissent increases. Incentives need not be explicitly coercive to shape behavior; they operate through structural alignment of reward and risk.

Fourth, institutional narratives may evolve to reinforce legitimacy independent of outcome. Language intended to signal care, integrity, or mission alignment can, under certain conditions, substitute for direct engagement with performance reality. Narrative reinforcement is not inherently deceptive; it becomes distortive when it replaces rather than reflects corrective feedback.

None of these conditions alone constitute Occupational Psychosis. The conditions represent structural variables. The phenomenon becomes more probable when such variables converge and reinforce one another over time.

From Drift to Normalization

Institutional distortion rarely appears abruptly. It usually unfolds gradually. Sociological analyses of organizations have long observed that deviation can become normalized when initial departures from standard practice do not immediately produce visible harm. Incremental adjustments, especially when rationalized as necessary adaptations, may accumulate into structural drift. When early signals are weak or ambiguous, institutions may interpret the absence of immediate failure as confirmation of stability.

Over time, the organization's internal definition of acceptable deviation may shift. Practices once considered temporary may become embedded. Feedback loops may narrow. Critical voices may exit or disengage. The system continues to function, often competently, while reflexive capacity diminishes.

This gradualism complicates recognition. Institutional actors may sincerely believe they are operating within normative boundaries even as structural conditions constrain corrective revision.

Authority and Reflexivity

Reflexivity, which is the capacity of a system to examine its assumptions, receive corrective information, and revise action in light of consequences is central to institutional stability.

Authority structures do not eliminate reflexivity; they organize it. Hierarchical systems exist in part to coordinate knowledge, clarify responsibility, and support decision-making under conditions of complexity.

However, when authority becomes insulated from meaningful correction, reflexive capacity may narrow. Authority insulation does not require malicious intent. It may arise through procedural layering, professional credentialing, risk management practices, or reputational caution. These mechanisms often originate as protective measures designed to ensure consistency and reduce institutional vulnerability. Yet when they accumulate without countervailing transparency, they can limit the system's ability to perceive and respond to emerging distortion. Occupational Psychosis therefore concerns impaired institutional reality-testing.

The analogy to clinical psychosis remains structural rather than diagnostic. Just as individual psychosis involves compromised differentiation between perception and external reality, institutional psychosis involves compromised differentiation between narrative coherence and operational reality. The analogy remains bounded and non-clinical.

The Function of Classification

The purpose of this volume is not to diagnose institutions but to classify recurring structural patterns. Classification precedes governance. Without shared vocabulary, structural drift remains difficult to articulate and therefore difficult to examine with analytic precision.

This chapter therefore marks the transition from conceptual definition to structural mapping. The chapters that follow examine the principal conditions through which manifestation becomes more probable within complex authority systems.

Each condition represents a structural variable rather than a diagnostic indicator. In isolation, these variables may reflect ordinary institutional functioning. It is their interaction and reinforcement over time that may constrain reflexivity and weaken corrective feedback.

Chapter two examines identity-role fusion, examining how professional identity can become structurally intertwined with institutional legitimacy. Subsequent chapters analyze authority insulation, metric substitution, incentive alignment, and narrative capture as distinct but interacting dynamics. Only after these structural conditions are clarified can institutional failure modes be systematically classified.

CHAPTER 2

IDENTITY-ROLE FUSION AND OCCUPATIONAL ENCLOSURE

Institutions depend upon professional identity. Strong professional identity is often essential for institutional coherence and ethical commitment. Role clarity enables coordination, expertise, and accountability. Without identifiable occupational roles, large-scale systems would struggle to function. Professional identification fosters commitment, ethical obligation, and shared standards of practice.

Identity-role alignment is not inherently problematic. It becomes structurally significant when alignment shifts toward fusion. Professional identification is a functional and often necessary feature of institutional stability; vulnerability arises only under compounded structural conditions.

Identity-Role Fusion

Identity role fusion occurs when occupational role and personal identity become increasingly indistinguishable. The professional function ceases to be something one performs and becomes central to how one understands oneself. Under such conditions, critique of role performance may be experienced not as procedural evaluation but as existential threat. Within the framework of Occupational Psychosis, identity-role fusion represents a structural precondition rather than a moral defect.

Organizational scholarship has long recognized the centrality of identity in professional life. Individuals derive meaning, belonging, and status from occupational membership. However, when identity investment intensifies without corresponding reflexive distance, the ability to differentiate between role critique and self-critique may narrow.

Fusion is not a psychological defect. It is a structural development shaped by institutional reinforcement. Systems reward loyalty, consistency, and narrative alignment. Over time, reinforcement may strengthen identification with the institution's moral framing, particularly where professional legitimacy is tied to mission orientation.

The structural concern is not identification itself, but diminished differentiation. When role becomes self, disconfirming information may threaten not only procedural performance but personal coherence. This dynamic can subtly shift incentives away from correction and toward preservation.

Occupational Enclosure

Occupational enclosure refers to the structural narrowing of interpretive boundaries within professional systems. As identity-role fusion intensifies, institutions may develop increasingly closed interpretive frameworks. Enclosure can take several forms:

- Credential insulation, where authority is confined to those within the professional boundary

- Normative homogeneity, where shared assumptions remain largely unchallenged

- Boundary reinforcement, where external critique is discounted as uninformed or misaligned

Such enclosure often develops as a protective mechanism. Professions establish boundaries to maintain standards, prevent dilution of expertise, and safeguard public trust. However, when boundary maintenance becomes resistant to reflexive challenge, enclosure may constrain corrective learning.

Occupational enclosure reduces exposure to alternative interpretive frameworks. Over time, systems may rely predominantly on internally validated narratives. External feedback may be filtered through pre-existing assumptions, narrowing the range of considered responses. Enclosure does not require secrecy or deliberate exclusion. It may arise gradually through specialization, credentialing, and professional socialization.

Professional Socialization and Reinforcement

Professional identity is shaped through training, accreditation, and peer recognition. Socialization processes transmit norms regarding appropriate conduct, interpretation of evidence, and ethical priorities. These processes stabilize professional practice and promote coherence.

Yet socialization can also reinforce interpretive convergence. When shared narratives are strongly internalized, dissent may appear as deviance rather than legitimate critique. Over time, this can reduce the permeability of professional boundaries. Institutional actors may not perceive enclosure because interpretive alignment feels natural and coherent. The narrowing of interpretive diversity often occurs incrementally.

From Fusion to Reflexive Constraint

Identity-role fusion and occupational enclosure do not produce distortion automatically. They become structurally significant when combined with additional variables-particularly authority insulation and incentive alignment.

When fused identity intersects with insulated authority, corrective signals may encounter resistance before they are fully evaluated. When incentives reward narrative stability, the cost of dissent increases further. Under these compounded conditions, reflexive capacity may narrow.

The structural pattern is cumulative rather than abrupt. Institutions may continue to function effectively across many domains while interpretive flexibility decreases in others. The analytic distinction that identity-role fusion and occupational enclosure are not moral failings is critical. They are structural developments that increase vulnerability to distortion under certain configurations. Within the framework of Occupational Psychosis, identity-role fusion functions as a precondition that increases vulnerability to institutional reality-testing impairment.

Identity-role fusion therefore represents a structural condition rather than a diagnostic indicator. In isolation it reflects ordinary institutional functioning within professional systems. Its analytic significance emerges only when interacting with additional structural conditions that shape institutional reflexivity. Chapter three examines authority insulation as a second variable within this broader configuration.

CHAPTER 3

AUTHORITY INSULATION AND REFLEXIVE COLLAPSE

Authority is indispensable to institutional life. Complex systems require decision hierarchies, role differentiation, and delegated responsibility. Authority structures coordinate action, allocate resources, and establish accountability. Without authority, institutional coherence deteriorates.

Authority insulation does not refer to the existence of hierarchy. It refers to the progressive narrowing of corrective exposure within authority structures. Authority insulation is not synonymous with authoritarianism; it describes structural filtering dynamics that may arise even within well-intentioned and procedurally compliant systems.

Authority and Feedback

Healthy authority systems depend on reflexivity which is the capacity to receive, interpret, and act upon corrective information. Reflexivity requires permeability between decision levels and operational realities. It depends upon feedback channels that transmit disconfirming signals without excessive distortion.

Authority insulation develops when these feedback channels narrow or become asymmetrical. Insulation may arise through procedural layering, credential boundaries, reputational caution, or risk management practices. Each of these mechanisms often originates as a stabilizing measure. Formal review processes protect against arbitrary decision-making. Credentialing protects expertise. Risk management reduces liability. Yet when such mechanisms accumulate without counterbalancing transparency, they can reduce exposure to corrective input. The result is not necessarily concealment, but filtering.

Information may travel upward selectively. Negative signals may be reframed as anomalies. Operational concerns may be interpreted through existing loyalty or alignment frameworks rather than as corrective data. Over time, informational asymmetry can widen the decision authority and lived institutional conditions. Within the framework of Occupational Psychosis, authority insulation is analyzed as a conditional structural variable rather than a moral judgment about leaders or institutions.

Structural Sources of Insulation

Authority insulation can develop through several structural dynamics:

Hierarchical Distance

As organizational layers increase, interpretive mediation increases. Information transmitted upward may be condensed, reformulated, or aligned with perceived expectations. This does not require deception; it reflects the sociology of communication within hierarchy.

Credential Gatekeeping

When interpretive authority is confined to credentialed actors, external critique may be discounted structurally rather than substantively. Expertise is necessary; exclusivity becomes distortive only when it forecloses reflexive examination.

Reputational Sensitivity

Institutions concerned with legitimacy may regulate internal discourse to avoid reputational volatility. Protective caution may unintentionally constrain open corrective dialogue.

Procedural Formalization

Highly formalized systems may privilege documented processes over emergent signals. When procedures become ends in themselves, reflexive revision may slow.

None of these dynamics is inherently pathological. They are structural features of modern organizations. Insulation becomes consequential only when compounded by additional constraints on reflexivity and reinforced by interacting structural conditions.

Reflexive Collapse

Reflexive collapse refers to the progressive weakening of institutional self-correction. It does not imply absence of reflection. Rather, it denotes a narrowing of acceptable interpretation within the system.

In reflexively healthy systems, authority is periodically exposed to disconfirming information. Revision is possible without destabilizing identity or legitimacy. In reflexively constrained systems, correction becomes increasingly costly. Alternative interpretations may be filtered through pre-existing alignment expectations, narrowing the scope of permissible critique.

Reflexive collapse is rarely abrupt. It unfolds gradually through cumulative filtering. Leaders may continue to perceive themselves as responsive while structural barriers constrain the type and scope of information that reaches decision thresholds.

Over time, institutional narratives may become more stable even as interpretive diversity decreases. Apparent coherence can coexist with diminished corrective capacity. Within Occupational Psychosis, reflexive collapse is understood as an impairment of institutional reality-testing capacity under specific compounded structural conditions.

Insulation and Identity Interaction

Authority insulation interacts with identity-role fusion in compounding ways.

Where identity and role are tightly fused, insulated authority structures may interpret critique as destabilizing rather than informative. Where authority is insulated, fused identity may face fewer corrective challenges. The interaction amplifies structural vulnerability.

This interaction remains conditional. Authority insulation does not produce distortion independently. It increases exposure only when combined with identity fusion, incentive alignment pressures, and narrative reinforcement mechanisms.

Understanding insulation as structural rather than moral is essential. Authority systems often evolve protective layers in response to legitimate risk, regulatory complexity, or scale. The analytic task is not to eliminate authority but to clarify how insulation may constrain reflexivity under certain configurations. The following chapter examines how performance measurement systems may further interact with insulated authority structures.

Authority insulation thus describes a structural feature of institutional design rather than a categorical failure of governance. Hierarchical mediation and professional filtering often support coordination and stability. The dynamics described here become analytically significant only when combined with other structural conditions that limit corrective feedback. The next chapter examines metric substitution as another variable within this evolving configuration.

CHAPTER 4

METRIC SUBSTITUTION AND PERFORMANCE SUBSTITUTION

Measurement is essential to institutional functioning. Complex systems require indicators to allocate resources, evaluate outcomes, and maintain accountability. Metrics translate activity into comparable signals. Institutions struggle to coordinate scale without measurement.

Metric substitution does not refer to the presence of measurement. It refers to the progressive displacement of underlying performance reality by its indicators. Measurement is not the problem under analysis; vulnerability arises only when proxy alignment weakens without corrective recalibration.

Indicators and Proxies

All institutional metrics are proxies. They represent selected dimensions of performance rather than performance in its entirety. Proxies are necessary because direct observation of all outcomes is impractical in large systems. However, proxy measures carry structural risk when they become detached from the phenomena they were designed to represent.

Metric substitution occurs when indicators begin to function as stand-ins for performance rather than as signals about performance. Systems may optimize for measured outputs even if underlying outcomes remain unchanged or deteriorate when proxy alignment weakens.

This dynamic is well documented in organizational research. Performance indicators influence behavior. Once an indicator becomes consequential in that it is linked to funding, advancement, reputation, or compliance, it shapes decision priorities. Under certain conditions, optimization of the indicator may displace the original objective.

Within the framework of Occupational Psychosis, metric substitution is understood as a structural shift in which measurement coherence supersedes performance coherence. It functions as a compounding structural variable rather than a critique of quantification itself.

Structural Drivers of Substitution

Metric substitution may emerge gradually through cumulative institutional adaptation:

Incentive Coupling

When advancement or legitimacy is tied tightly to measurable outputs, actors rationally orient behavior toward those outputs. The stronger the coupling, the greater the risk is that proxy optimization eclipses the underlying purpose.

Complexity Reduction

Metrics simplify reality. Simplification is necessary for coordination, yet overreliance on simplified indicators may narrow interpretive attention.

Audit Culture

Formal accountability structures often privilege documented compliance. When compliance verification becomes the dominant evaluative mechanism, symbolic adherence may substitute for substantive engagement.

Reputational Visibility

Public-facing metrics may become central to institutional identity. Highly visible indicators can shape narrative coherence, particularly where institutional legitimacy depends on comparative performance. None of these drivers are inherently distortive. Measurement supports accountability. The analytic concern arises when proxy fidelity declines without detection.

Performance Substitution

Performance substitution occurs when institutional actors equate favorable metrics with satisfactory outcomes even when other signals suggest emerging deviation. Substitution may be unintentional. It often reflects reliance on available indicators rather than deliberate manipulation.

The distinction between metric use and metric substitution is therefore structural rather than moral. Institutions depend on measurable indicators. Substitution becomes relevant when alternative feedback mechanisms weaken, narrowing the interpretive range through which performance is assessed.

When combined with authority insulation, metric substitution can reinforce informational asymmetry. Decision-makers may rely on aggregated indicators that appear stable while operational realities become more variable. When combined with identity-role fusion, metric defense may intensify because indicators support institutional self-concept.

Within Occupational Psychosis, metric substitution increases vulnerability only when reinforced by additional structural preconditions. It does not independently produce distortion.

Metric substitution often develops without overt intent. Institutions refine indicators to improve precision. Over time, successive refinements may prioritize measurability over representational breadth. As attention converges on quantified outputs, unmeasured dimensions may recede from consideration.

Drift becomes difficult to detect when proxy success persists. Favorable indicators can reinforce institutional confidence, even if peripheral signals suggest narrowing interpretive scope. Because measurement provides apparent objectivity, metric stability may be interpreted as performance stability.

Metric substitution represents a structural tendency that may arise within systems that rely on quantitative indicators to coordinate performance. Metrics often enhance accountability and clarity. Their distortive potential emerges only when measurement substitutes for, rather than complements, evaluative judgment.

The structural concern is not quantification itself. It is the displacement of performance reality by its representation under compounded structural conditions. This analysis identifies structural exposure but does not prescribe measurement redesign or corrective governance mechanisms. The next chapter examines how incentive alignment may intensify these dynamics.

CHAPTER 5

INCENTIVE ALIGNMENT AND MORAL DRIFT

Incentive structures are fundamental to institutional coordination. Organizations depend upon aligned rewards, recognition systems, advancement criteria, and reputational signals to guide behavior across scale. Incentives clarify priorities and shape decision thresholds. Institutions fragment without incentive alignment.

Incentive alignment does not refer to corruption or manipulation. It refers to the structural coupling between institutional rewards and the specific forms of measurable, reputational, or procedural performance. The analytic concern arises when incentive systems progressively privilege narrative stability relative to corrective adaptation.

Incentives as Structural Signals

Incentives communicate value. They signal what behaviors, outcomes, and interpretations are rewarded or advanced. Because institutional actors respond rationally to reward structures, incentives often shape behavior more powerfully than mission statements.

Incentive alignment becomes structurally consequential when the criteria for advancement or recognition narrow interpretive flexibility. The cost of deviation increases when actors perceive that career progression, funding stability, or reputational standing depends upon preserving particular outcomes or narratives.

This dynamic does not require overt pressure. It may operate through subtle signals such as performance evaluation frameworks, promotion standards, funding renewal criteria, public recognition systems, and compliance scoring.

Each of these mechanisms may operate legitimately. The structural question is whether the incentive environment preserves space for corrective dissent or progressively narrows it. Within the framework of Occupational Psychosis, incentive alignment functions as a compounding structural condition. It increases vulnerability when rewards are more consistently attached to stability than to reflexive revision.

From Alignment to Drift

Moral drift does not imply ethical collapse. It refers to gradual recalibration of institutional thresholds regarding what is considered acceptable, sufficient, or successful. The term "moral drift" is used descriptively to indicate threshold recalibration, not to allege moral failure or ethical misconduct.

As incentive systems reinforce particular outputs, interpretations of adequacy may shift incrementally. Practices once viewed as provisional may become normalized. Deviations may be reclassified as tolerable variance. Over time, standards may adjust to reflect what is consistently rewarded.

Drift often occurs without deliberate intent. Institutional actors may sincerely believe they are maintaining integrity while gradually adjusting evaluative criteria in response to incentive structures. Because adjustment unfolds incrementally, it may not trigger immediate concern.

The concept parallels longstanding sociological observations that goal displacement can emerge when means become ends. Mission interpretation may adapt accordingly when procedural compliance or indicator success becomes the primary pathway to institutional reward.

Within Occupational Psychosis, moral drift refers specifically to incremental threshold adjustment under incentive reinforcement, not to broad ethical decline. It functions as a structural recalibration that becomes consequential only when compounded by additional preconditions.

Interaction with Prior Preconditions

Incentive alignment interacts with identity through role fusion, authority insulation, and metric substitution in reinforcing ways. When identity and role are fused, incentive protection of institutional narrative may be experienced as protection of self. When authority structures are insulated, incentive signals may travel downward more effectively than corrective feedback travels upward. When metric substitution has occurred, incentives may attach to proxy success rather than underlying performance. These interactions increase structural exposure, but do not guarantee distortion.

Incentive systems are indispensable to institutional functioning. The analytic concern is not their presence but their coupling. The probability of drift increases when reward structures consistently privilege narrative stability, metric coherence, or procedural compliance over reflexive recalibration.

Incentive alignment therefore reflects a foundational feature of institutional coordination rather than an inherent source of distortion. Incentives shape behavior in all complex systems. Their structural implications become analytically significant only when interacting with additional dynamics that constrain corrective revision.

This analysis identifies structural exposure rather than prescriptive reform. This chapter does not propose incentive restructuring or governance intervention. Questions of incentive redesign, governance safeguards, and corrective architecture fall beyond the scope of this volume. The last chapter of Part I examines how narrative capture and legitimacy protection may consolidate these dynamics.

CHAPTER 6

NARRATIVE CAPTURE AND LEGITIMACY PROTECTION

Institutions depend upon narrative coherence. Mission statements, professional codes, strategic plans, and public communications articulate purpose and guide interpretation. Narrative provides continuity across leadership transitions, contextualizes performance outcomes, and sustains collective identity.

Narrative capture does not refer to deliberate misrepresentation. It refers to the progressive alignment of institutional interpretation with internally reinforced narratives in ways that narrow interpretive flexibility. Narrative capture does not imply deception or intentional concealment; it describes structural interpretive narrowing under compounded conditions.

Narrative as Institutional Infrastructure

All institutions operate through shared interpretive frameworks. These frameworks organize meaning, coordinate action, and stabilize expectations. Without narrative coherence, institutions fragment into competing interpretations of purpose and success.

Narratives are therefore functional. They allow institutions to maintain legitimacy across changing conditions. Legitimacy itself is relational; it depends on alignment between institutional conduct and stakeholder expectations. The structural concern arises when narrative coherence becomes increasingly insulated from disconfirming signals.

Within the framework of Occupational Psychosis, narrative capture refers specifically to the dominance of internally reinforced meaning frameworks over corrective feedback under compounded structural preconditions. It functions as a compounding structural variable rather than a claim of intentional distortion.

Mechanisms of Narrative Reinforcement

Narrative capture may develop gradually through routine institutional processes:

Repetition and Internalization

Repeated articulation of mission language reinforces interpretive alignment. Over time, narrative may become reflexively invoked as explanatory closure.

Symbolic Consistency

Visual branding, formal reporting structures, and standardized communication practices strengthen narrative stability.

Selective Amplification

Positive performance indicators may be integrated prominently into institutional storytelling, while ambiguous or corrective signals receive less interpretive emphasis.

Legitimacy Defense

Institutions facing reputational scrutiny may emphasize narrative continuity to preserve stakeholder confidence.

Each of these mechanisms may serve legitimate stabilizing purposes. Narrative reinforcement becomes structurally significant when it constrains interpretive revision.

Legitimacy Protection and Threshold Adjustment

Legitimacy protection is not inherently distortive. Institutions must defend credibility in order to function. However, when legitimacy maintenance becomes tightly coupled to identity-role fusion, authority insulation, metric substitution, and incentive alignment, interpretive narrowing may intensify.

In such conditions, corrective information may be evaluated primarily in relation to its perceived impact on institutional legitimacy. Signals that challenge narrative coherence may encounter higher interpretive thresholds.

This dynamic does not require intentional concealment. It may arise through rational efforts to preserve stability during uncertainty. Yet the cumulative effect can be reduced permeability between external feedback and internal interpretation.

Within Occupational Psychosis, narrative capture represents the consolidation phase of structural preconditions. It describes the increasing dominance of internally reinforced meaning frameworks under compounded conditions.

Narrative Stability and Reflexive Constraint

Stable narratives are essential to institutional continuity. The analytic concern is not stability itself, but rigidity under conditions requiring recalibration.

When narrative coherence becomes resistant to revision, reflexive capacity may narrow further. Corrective feedback may be interpreted through pre-existing explanatory frames, reducing the likelihood of substantive adjustment.

Narrative capture does not imply falsification. It describes a structural dynamic in which interpretive frameworks become progressively self-reinforcing. Under compounded structural conditions, narrative may function as both explanatory system and protective boundary.

This chapter concludes Part I by clarifying how identity-role fusion, authority insulation, metric substitution, incentive alignment, and narrative reinforcement may interact. Individually, each condition may serve functional purposes. In combination, they increase the probability that institutional reality-testing becomes constrained.

Narrative coherence plays an essential role in sustaining institutional identity and legitimacy. Narrative capture therefore represents a structural dynamic rather than a diagnostic determination. Its significance emerges only when narrative reinforcement begins to substitute for corrective engagement with operational reality.

The structural preconditions outlined in Part I are foundational features of modern institutional design. Their presence alone does not constitute dysfunction. They become analytically significant only when compounded and reinforced without sufficient reflexive counterbalance. The analysis that follows classifies observable failure modes that may emerge under such compounded conditions. It does not evaluate specific institutions nor prescribe reform. The following sections turn from structural preconditions to the classification of institutional failure modes.

PART II

INSTITUTIONAL FAILURE MODES

CHAPTER 7

EPISTEMIC NARROWING

Epistemic narrowing refers to the progressive constriction of interpretive range within an institutional system. It describes a reduction in the diversity of perspectives, evidentiary standards, or interpretive frameworks through which information is evaluated. Narrowing does not imply absence of knowledge; it indicates selective consolidation of acceptable knowledge.

Epistemic narrowing is not a claim about political ideology or intentional manipulation; it describes a structural reduction in interpretive variance that may arise through ordinary institutional consolidation.

Within the framework of Occupational Psychosis, epistemic narrowing functions as an observable failure mode that may emerge when structural preconditions of identity-role fusion, authority insulation, metric substitution, incentive alignment, and narrative capture interact without sufficient reflexive counterbalance. In this canon, epistemic narrowing is analyzed as an institutional sensemaking constraint rather than an individual cognitive bias.

Institutions require shared interpretive standards in order to coordinate action. Epistemic coherence is necessary for decision-making. Narrowing becomes analytically significant when interpretive boundaries contract in ways that limit exposure to disconfirming information.

Structural Emergence

Epistemic narrowing rarely appears abruptly. It often develops gradually as institutional systems reinforce particular explanatory frames. When identity-role fusion intensifies, interpretive alignment may become closely associated with professional legitimacy. Alternative perspectives may be regarded as misaligned rather than exploratory.

As authority structures become insulated, the range of perspectives that reach decision thresholds may diminish. When metric substitution privileges quantifiable indicators, unmeasured dimensions of performance may receive less interpretive attention. Incentive alignment may further reinforce conformity to prevailing frameworks. Narrative capture may consolidate internally coherent explanations, reducing interpretive permeability.

Under compounded conditions, interpretive diversity may narrow without explicit exclusion and without deliberate intent. Institutional actors may sincerely perceive their interpretive range as adequate, even as certain forms of evidence receive diminishing consideration.

Epistemic narrowing is not synonymous with censorship or suppression. It describes a structural pattern in which institutional sensemaking becomes increasingly self-reinforcing.

Interaction With Other Modes

Epistemic narrowing may co-occur with other failure modes. When interpretive range contracts, feedback suppression may intensify, as alternative signals struggle to gain institutional traction. Incentivized conformity may reinforce alignment with prevailing frameworks.

Symbolic compliance may expand, as formal adherence to standards substitutes for interpretive revision. Authority inflation may be reinforced, as interpretive legitimacy concentrates within fewer nodes. These modes are analytically distinct but structurally interdependent. Epistemic narrowing rarely operates in isolation.

Boundary Clarification

Epistemic narrowing does not imply intellectual incapacity or intentional exclusion. Institutions must reduce complexity to function. The analytic concern is not interpretive coherence but interpretive rigidity under conditions requiring revision.

Nor does epistemic narrowing imply ideological uniformity. It may arise within systems of diverse political or cultural orientation. The phenomenon concerns structural contraction of acceptable interpretive pathways rather than the content of belief.

Within Occupational Psychosis, epistemic narrowing refers specifically to reduction in institutional reality-testing range under compounded structural conditions. It is not equivalent to disagreement, debate limitation, or temporary strategic focus.

This chapter classifies epistemic narrowing as a structural failure mode for analytic purposes. It does not constitute institutional diagnosis, nor does it prescribe corrective intervention or evaluative criteria. The presence of interpretive coherence does not imply dysfunction; narrowing becomes analytically significant only when compounded with additional structural preconditions.

The narrowing of institutional knowledge rarely occurs in isolation. When systems begin to privilege certain interpretations of reality while excluding others, the range of acceptable understanding gradually contracts. Over time, this epistemic narrowing reshapes what organizations consider credible, legitimate, or even thinkable.

Yet narrowing alone does not fully explain how distorted institutional perceptions persist. For epistemic constraint to become stable, systems must also limit the corrective signals that might challenge it. Information that contradicts dominant narratives, performance claims, or leadership assumptions must be filtered, ignored, or discouraged.

This dynamic introduces the next pattern of institutional distortion. As epistemic boundaries tighten, the mechanisms that normally allow organizations to detect error and adjust course begin to weaken. Signals that might reveal misalignment, harm, or failure are muted before they can influence decision-making.

The result is not simply a narrower understanding of reality, but a system increasingly insulated from the feedback required to maintain alignment with it.

The following chapter examines this process of feedback suppression and the conditions under which institutions lose the capacity to receive, interpret, and act upon corrective information.

CHAPTER 8

FEEDBACK SUPPRESSION

Feedback suppression refers to the attenuation, delay, reinterpretation, or procedural neutralization of corrective signals within an institutional system. It describes what occurs when disconfirming information is generated but fails to meaningfully influence interpretive or decision thresholds.

Whereas authority insulation describes structural filtering within hierarchical architecture, feedback suppression refers to the dampening of corrective signals after they emerge. The two phenomena may co-occur but are analytically distinct. Authority insulation concerns positional distance while feedback suppression concerns signal attenuation.

Feedback suppression does not imply intentional silencing or punitive response; it may arise through routine procedural or interpretive prioritization.

Within the framework of Occupational Psychosis, feedback suppression refers specifically to reduced structural influence of corrective signals at the institutional level. It functions as an observable failure mode that may arise under compounded structural preconditions.

Structural Emergence

Institutions generate feedback continuously. Performance reports, stakeholder responses, operational irregularities, and internal critique all function as corrective inputs. Feedback suppression becomes analytically significant when such inputs lose their capacity to alter interpretation or action.

Suppression may develop through several structural dynamics. Corrective signals may be reframed as anomalies rather than indicators. Procedural channels may exist formally yet operate with extended delay, reducing urgency. Dissenting perspectives may be redirected into review processes that diffuse their impact. Ambiguous data may be interpreted preferentially through prevailing explanatory frameworks.

These dynamics do not require coercion and may occur without deliberate intent. They may emerge from incentive alignment pressures, narrative coherence protection, or identity-role fusion. Institutional actors may sincerely believe that corrective input has been addressed even as its structural influence diminishes. Feedback suppression thus describes a systemic reduction in the effective weight of disconfirming information.

Interaction With Other Modes

Feedback suppression frequently interacts with epistemic narrowing. As interpretive range contracts, the probability that corrective signals are reinterpreted rather than integrated increases. Metric substitution may intensify suppression when unfavorable signals fall outside measurable indicators. Incentivized conformity (Chapter 9) may further dampen dissent when deviation carries reputational cost. Narrative capture may frame corrective input as destabilizing rather than informative.

Authority insulation may increase the likelihood that suppressed signals fail to reach decision thresholds, yet suppression can also occur in relatively flat systems where informal norms discourage sustained critique. These failure modes are analytically distinct but structurally interdependent.

Boundary Clarification

Feedback suppression does not imply censorship, retaliation, or formal prohibition of dissent. Institutions may exhibit suppression even when channels for feedback remain technically available. The analytic concern is not the presence of communication pathways but the effective influence of corrective input.

Nor does feedback suppression imply institutional incapacity. Institutions routinely triage information. Prioritization is necessary. Suppression becomes analytically significant when disconfirming signals are consistently attenuated under compounded structural conditions.

Within Occupational Psychosis, feedback suppression refers specifically to diminished institutional responsiveness to corrective information. It is not equivalent to temporary delay, strategic discretion, or disagreement.

This chapter classifies feedback suppression as a structural failure mode for analytic purposes. It does not constitute institutional diagnosis, nor does it prescribe reporting reform, governance safeguards, or compliance redesign. The presence of selective information processing does not imply dysfunction; suppression becomes analytically significant only when compounded with additional structural preconditions.

When feedback mechanisms weaken, institutions lose one of their most important safeguards against distortion. Systems that can no longer reliably receive or interpret corrective signals become increasingly insulated from the consequences of their own decisions. Over time, misalignment with reality is not only tolerated but normalized.

Yet the suppression of feedback does not occur passively. For distorted conditions to persist across an organization, individuals must learn, implicitly or explicitly, that certain observations, concerns, or forms of dissent are unwelcome. Signals that challenge prevailing narratives are not simply ignored; they are gradually discouraged.

This discouragement often emerges through subtle but powerful institutional incentives. Advancement, recognition, and professional legitimacy become tied to alignment with established interpretations of success, effectiveness, or moral purpose. Individuals who question those interpretations may encounter reputational risk, stalled advancement, or social exclusion, while those who reinforce them are rewarded.

Under such conditions, organizational behavior begins to shift. Silence becomes safer than critique, agreement becomes more advantageous than scrutiny, and conformity becomes the rational response to institutional pressures.

The next chapter examines how these dynamics consolidate into incentivized conformity, a pattern in which systems actively reward alignment with dominant narratives while discouraging the forms of dissent and inquiry necessary for institutional self-correction.

CHAPTER 9

INCENTIVIZED CONFORMITY

Incentivized conformity refers to the adaptive behavioral pattern that may emerge when institutional reward structures consistently privilege alignment with prevailing interpretations, indicators, or narratives. Whereas incentive alignment describes the structural coupling between rewards and institutional priorities, incentivized conformity concerns the patterned response of actors within that reward environment.

Alignment is architectural and conformity is adaptive. Incentivized conformity does not imply ideological enforcement or uniformity of belief; it describes patterned behavioral adaptation to institutional reward signals.

Within the framework of Occupational Psychosis, incentivized conformity is analyzed at the institutional level of reward-structured adaptation rather than interpersonal pressure dynamics. It functions as an observable failure mode that may arise when deviation becomes structurally costly and alignment becomes structurally advantageous. It does not require coercion, explicit instruction, or overt sanction. Conformity may develop through rational adjustment to incentive signals.

Structural Emergence

Institutions communicate expectations through evaluation systems, promotion pathways, reputational signals, and resource allocation patterns. When these signals consistently reward interpretive alignment and procedural adherence, actors adapt accordingly.

Incentivized conformity may manifest as anticipatory alignment. Institutional participants may calibrate language, analysis, or reporting practices to align with established priorities. Over time, behavioral adjustment may precede explicit instruction. Self-regulation becomes embedded within professional practice.

This dynamic differs from feedback suppression. Suppression concerns what happens to corrective signals after they are expressed. Incentivized conformity concerns the reduced likelihood that such signals are generated in the first place. When deviation carries structural cost, actors may internalize alignment expectations.

Conformity in this context is not inherently irrational or unethical. It reflects adaptive response to structured reward systems. The analytic concern arises when adaptive alignment narrows interpretive diversity and reduces the generation of corrective input under compounded structural conditions.

Interaction With Other Modes

Incentivized conformity frequently interacts with epistemic narrowing and feedback suppression.

As interpretive range contracts, the cost of divergence increases. Conformity may reinforce narrowing by reducing exposure to alternative perspectives. When conformity reduces dissent generation, feedback suppression mechanisms require less overt activation. Metric substitution may further intensify conformity if measurable indicators are closely tied to reward structures. Narrative capture may legitimize alignment by framing it as mission fidelity.

Authority insulation may amplify the perceived distance between decision-makers and operational actors, increasing the perceived risk of deviation. Conversely, conformity may persist even in decentralized systems when informal reward norms signal strong alignment expectations. These failure modes are analytically distinct yet structurally reinforcing.

Boundary Clarification

Incentivized conformity does not imply forced compliance or absence of independent judgment. Institutions require shared standards and coordinated behavior. Conformity becomes analytically significant when adaptive alignment consistently reduces the generation of corrective variance under compounded structural preconditions.

Nor does incentivized conformity imply ideological uniformity. The phenomenon concerns structural adaptation to reward signals rather than the specific content of belief or value orientation. Within Occupational Psychosis, incentivized conformity refers specifically to patterned behavioral adjustment under incentive reinforcement at the institutional level. It is not equivalent to collegial agreement, professional consensus, or temporary strategic focus.

This chapter classifies incentivized conformity as a structural failure mode for analytic purposes. It does not constitute institutional diagnosis, nor does it propose cultural redesign, leadership intervention, or incentive restructuring. The presence of coordinated alignment does not imply dysfunction; conformity becomes analytically significant only when compounded with additional structural preconditions.

As incentives begin to favor alignment over inquiry, conformity gradually becomes embedded in institutional behavior. Individuals learn that professional stability, recognition, and advancement are more reliably achieved by reinforcing established narratives than by questioning them. Over time, this dynamic reshapes not only decision-making but also how organizations present themselves to the outside world.

When conformity becomes institutionalized, the appearance of responsibility or responsiveness often takes precedence over the underlying reality of corrective action. Systems may continue to acknowledge problems, adopt new language, or announce reforms, yet these responses frequently remain confined to symbolic gestures rather than substantive change.

This shift marks an important transformation in how institutional distortion is maintained. Incentivized conformity stabilizes internal alignment around prevailing narratives, while outward-facing signals are crafted to demonstrate compliance with professional, ethical, or regulatory expectations. The organization appears responsive, accountable, and aligned with accepted standards even as the underlying conditions that generated concern remain largely unchanged.

In this way, the pressures that reward conformity also encourage institutions to substitute symbolic acts for structural correction. Declarations of reform, revised policies, or public commitments can function less as mechanisms of change and more as signals of legitimacy.

Chapter ten examines this pattern of symbolic compliance and the conditions under which organizations increasingly rely on performative responses that preserve institutional credibility without meaningfully altering underlying practices.

CHAPTER 10

SYMBOLIC COMPLIANCE

Symbolic compliance refers to patterned adherence to formal procedures, policies, standards, or reporting requirements in ways that prioritize visible conformity over substantive engagement with underlying institutional purpose.

Whereas metric substitution concerns the displacement of performance reality by its indicators, symbolic compliance refers to the performative enactment of those indicators or rules when substantive alignment becomes secondary. Metric substitution operates at the level of representation; symbolic compliance operates at the level of behavior.

Symbolic compliance does not imply fraudulent reporting or intentional misrepresentation; it describes structural decoupling that may arise even within lawful and well-intentioned systems.

Within the framework of Occupational Psychosis, symbolic compliance is analyzed as a compounded manifestation of metric substitution and incentivized conformity under institutional identity consolidation. It functions as an observable failure mode that may emerge under compounded structural preconditions.

Structural Emergence

Institutions depend on formal procedures to maintain coordination, accountability, and legitimacy. Compliance structures provide traceability, auditability, and standardized expectations. Under stable conditions, procedural adherence supports institutional coherence.

Symbolic compliance becomes analytically significant when adherence to formal requirements begins to substitute for engagement with underlying objectives.

This shift may develop gradually. When metric substitution privileges quantifiable indicators, and incentive alignment rewards procedural conformity, actors may rationally prioritize demonstrable compliance. Narrative capture may further reinforce visible alignment as evidence of institutional integrity. Under these compounded conditions, procedural performance may assume heightened institutional importance.

Symbolic compliance does not require falsification of records or fabrication of outcomes. It may arise through ritualization. Reports may be completed thoroughly while underlying conditions remain substantively unchanged. Policies may be followed formally while interpretive engagement narrows. Documentation may demonstrate adherence even when adaptive revision would be warranted.

The analytic concern is not the existence of compliance systems but the increasing divergence between procedural demonstration and substantive effect.

Interaction With Other Modes

Symbolic compliance frequently interacts with metric substitution and incentivized conformity.

When proxy indicators are treated as performance reality, adherence to those indicators becomes institutionally salient. Incentivized conformity may encourage anticipatory procedural alignment. Feedback suppression may reduce the likelihood that substantive concerns disrupt formal compliance processes. Epistemic narrowing may limit interpretive attention to documented adherence rather than emergent conditions.

Authority insulation may further attenuate the visibility of divergence between procedural performance and operational reality. These modes remain analytically distinct but structurally reinforcing.

Boundary Clarification

Symbolic compliance does not imply institutional dishonesty or moral failure. Institutions must formalize procedures to function. The analytic concern arises when procedural adherence becomes sufficient evidence of adequacy, independent of substantive outcomes.

Nor does symbolic compliance imply regulatory excess or bureaucratic inefficiency. It may occur in diverse institutional forms, including highly decentralized or mission-driven organizations. The phenomenon concerns structural ritualization rather than ideological orientation.

Within Occupational Psychosis, symbolic compliance refers specifically to patterned behavioral emphasis on procedural conformity under compounded structural conditions. It is not equivalent to ordinary documentation, policy adherence, or lawful compliance.

This chapter classifies symbolic compliance as a structural failure mode for analytic purposes. It does not constitute institutional diagnosis, nor does it prescribe audit redesign, regulatory modification, or compliance restructuring. The presence of formalized procedures does not imply dysfunction; symbolic compliance becomes analytically significant only when compounded with additional structural preconditions.

Symbolic compliance allows institutions to maintain the appearance of responsibility while leaving underlying conditions largely unchanged. By adopting the language of reform, accountability, or ethical commitment, organizations can signal responsiveness to internal or external concerns without engaging in the deeper structural changes those concerns may require. In this way, performative alignment becomes a stabilizing mechanism, preserving legitimacy even as meaningful correction is deferred.

Over time, however, the repeated reliance on symbolic responses has additional consequences. When institutional credibility is sustained through appearances rather than outcomes, authority itself can begin to expand beyond its original basis. Leaders, professions, or organizations may continue to receive trust, deference, and legitimacy even as the processes that normally constrain authority (evidence, feedback, and demonstrable results) grow weaker.

Under these conditions, authority becomes less tightly linked to performance or accountability and more closely associated with status, narrative control, or institutional identity. The capacity to define what counts as success, legitimacy, or responsible action may increasingly rest with those already occupying positions of influence.

This dynamic introduces the next pattern of institutional distortion. As symbolic compliance preserves the outward legitimacy of systems experiencing internal misalignment, authority can gradually detach from the conditions that once justified it. Authority expands not through demonstrated effectiveness but through the maintenance of institutional narratives that sustain trust and deference.

Chapter 11 examines this process of authority inflation and the ways in which institutional systems can accumulate and exercise increasing authority even as the mechanisms that normally discipline and constrain it begin to erode.

CHAPTER 11

AUTHORITY INFLATION

Authority inflation refers to the progressive amplification, centralization, or symbolic magnification of institutional authority under compounded structural conditions. Whereas authority insulation describes structural buffering within hierarchical architecture, authority inflation refers to the expansion or elevation of authority legitimacy and interpretive centrality beyond proportionate constraint.

Authority insulation concerns informational distance. Authority inflation concerns interpretive dominance. Authority inflation does not imply normative judgment regarding centralized governance; it describes structural amplification under specific compounded conditions.

Within the framework of Occupational Psychosis, authority inflation is analyzed as a compounded manifestation of interpretive consolidation under attenuated feedback conditions. It functions as an observable failure mode that may emerge when identity-role fusion, feedback attenuation, incentivized conformity, metric substitution, and narrative capture converge. It does not imply authoritarian intent, coercive governance, or ideological consolidation. Rather, it describes structural amplification of authority legitimacy under conditions of reduced corrective permeability.

Authority inflation is not inherently dysfunctional. Institutions require stable authority structures to coordinate action. The analytic concern arises when authority centrality expands in ways that diminish recalibration capacity under compounded structural conditions.

Structural Emergence

Institutions allocate authority to coordinate decision-making, maintain accountability, and stabilize expectations. Under ordinary conditions, authority operates within the distributed constraints of procedural checks, professional norms, stakeholder scrutiny, and informational feedback loops. Authority inflation may develop gradually when these constraints weaken or become unevenly distributed.

As epistemic narrowing reduces interpretive variance, authority judgments may encounter fewer countervailing perspectives. Feedback suppression may attenuate corrective signals before they meaningfully alter decision thresholds. Incentivized conformity may reduce upward challenge. Narrative capture may reinforce authority as the stabilizing interpreter of institutional purpose. Metric substitution may further legitimize authority through performance indicators that reinforce prevailing interpretations.

Under such compounded conditions, authority may become increasingly central to institutional meaning-making. Decisions may acquire heightened symbolic weight. Institutional identity may become closely aligned with authority interpretation. Legitimacy may consolidate upward even in the absence of formal expansion of power.

Authority inflation does not require explicit power acquisition or procedural revision. It may occur through interpretive consolidation and symbolic reinforcement.

Interaction With Other Modes

Authority inflation frequently interacts with epistemic narrowing, incentivized conformity, and symbolic compliance. As authority legitimacy consolidates, interpretive divergence may appear increasingly misaligned rather than exploratory. Incentivized conformity may intensify as alignment with central authority becomes structurally advantageous. Symbolic compliance may reinforce authority by demonstrating visible adherence to its directives. Feedback suppression may reduce the transmission of corrective signals capable of recalibrating authority judgments.

Authority insulation may increase the probability that inflation stabilizes, yet insulation and inflation remain analytically distinct. Insulation concerns positional buffering; inflation concerns legitimacy amplification. These modes are structurally reinforcing but conceptually separable.

Boundary Clarification

Authority inflation does not imply unlawful expansion of jurisdiction, deliberate consolidation of power, or ideological extremity. The phenomenon concerns structural elevation of authority centrality within institutional interpretive systems.

Nor does authority inflation imply that authority itself is undesirable. Authority is necessary for institutional coherence. The analytic concern arises when authority becomes the primary or exclusive locus of interpretive validation under compounded structural preconditions.

Within Occupational Psychosis, authority inflation refers specifically to amplified legitimacy concentration and interpretive centrality at the institutional level. It is not equivalent to strong leadership, decisive governance, or efficient coordination.

This chapter classifies authority inflation as a structural failure mode for analytic purposes. It does not constitute institutional diagnosis, nor does it propose decentralization, redistribution of authority, or governance restructuring. The presence of centralized authority does not imply dysfunction; authority inflation becomes analytically significant only when compounded with additional structural preconditions.

As authority expands beyond its original evidentiary and performance-based foundations, institutions often acquire an additional form of protection from scrutiny. When authority becomes associated not only with expertise or role legitimacy but also with perceived moral standing, challenges to that authority can begin to carry social and professional risk.

This shift marks an important development in the dynamics of institutional distortion. Inflated authority does more than concentrate decision-making power; it also shapes how actions taken by those in authority are interpreted. Leaders, professions, or organizations widely perceived as serving benevolent or socially valuable purposes may increasingly benefit from presumptions of ethical intent. Their authority is not only accepted but morally reinforced.

Over time, this moral reinforcement can create conditions in which institutions draw legitimacy from the very values that make them difficult to question. Appeals to mission, service, or public good become powerful shields against critique, particularly in systems oriented toward care, guidance, or social responsibility. When authority and moral identity become closely intertwined, scrutiny may be interpreted not as necessary oversight but as misunderstanding, disloyalty, or opposition to the institution's stated purpose.

This dynamic introduces the next pattern of institutional distortion. As authority expands and becomes intertwined with moral identity, institutions may accumulate what can be described as moral credentials, signals of virtue that grant them increased latitude and reduced scrutiny.

The following chapter examines the phenomenon of moral credentialing and the conditions under which institutions draw upon reputational claims of ethical purpose to justify, excuse, or deflect attention from actions that might otherwise invite greater accountability.

CHAPTER 12

MORAL CREDENTIALING

Moral credentialing refers to the progressive accumulation and invocation of moral legitimacy claims that function to buffer institutional authority from recalibration under compounded structural conditions. It describes a structural dynamic in which established moral positioning becomes increasingly central to institutional self-understanding and external validation.

Moral credentialing does not imply insincerity, hypocrisy, or strategic deception. Institutions frequently undertake activities oriented towards ethical responsibility, social benefit, or public service. The analytic concern arises not from the presence of moral commitments, but from the structural role those commitments may assume within interpretive and legitimacy systems.

Within Occupational Psychosis, moral credentialing is analyzed at the level of institutional legitimacy structures rather than individual psychological moral licensing. The concept does not evaluate the moral content of institutional missions nor their substantive ethical commitments.

Whereas narrative capture concerns dominance of interpretive frameworks, and symbolic compliance concerns ritualized procedural adherence, moral credentialing concerns ethical-legitimacy consolidation. It operates at the level of moral self-authorization rather than narrative coherence or procedural performance.

Within the framework of Occupational Psychosis, moral credentialing functions as an observable failure mode that may emerge when authority inflation, incentivized conformity, symbolic compliance, and feedback attenuation converge.

It does not evaluate the substantive merit of institutional missions; it analyzes the structural use of moral legitimacy under attenuated corrective conditions.

Structural Emergence

Institutions frequently articulate moral commitments through mission statements, ethical codes, public accountability reports, and service orientation. These commitments provide normative grounding and public trust.

Moral credentialing becomes analytically significant when accumulated moral positioning begins to function as a stabilizing reference point against recalibration.

Under compounded structural conditions, prior moral achievements or declared commitments may acquire buffering properties. Institutional identity may become closely aligned with moral self-description. Feedback that challenges operational effectiveness may be evaluated in relation to perceived moral standing. Authority interpretations may be reinforced through invocation of institutional virtue or historical contribution.

This dynamic does not require misrepresentation. It may arise through sincere institutional confidence grounded in prior accomplishment. However, when moral legitimacy becomes structurally intertwined with interpretive validation, recalibration thresholds may rise. Moral credentialing thus describes a shift in which moral capital increasingly functions as interpretive insulation.

Interaction With Other Modes

Moral credentialing frequently interacts with authority inflation and narrative capture.

As authority legitimacy consolidates, moral positioning may reinforce interpretive centrality. Narrative capture may integrate moral identity into institutional self-description. Incentivized conformity may reduce internal critique when moral alignment is strongly valued. Symbolic compliance may provide visible affirmation of ethical commitments. Feedback suppression may attenuate signals that complicate moral self-understanding.

These interactions do not imply ethical failure. Rather, they describe how moral legitimacy can become structurally entangled with authority consolidation under compounded preconditions.

Moral credentialing rarely operates independently; it tends to appear in later stages of the structural cascade.

Boundary Clarification

Moral credentialing does not imply moral misconduct, ethical corruption, or bad faith. Institutions often pursue socially beneficial aims and maintain genuine ethical commitments. The analytic concern is not moral aspiration but structural overreliance on moral positioning as a stabilizing reference point under reduced corrective permeability.

Nor does moral credentialing imply ideological extremity or partisan alignment. The phenomenon concerns structural legitimacy buffering rather than substantive political orientation.

Within Occupational Psychosis, moral credentialing refers specifically to the increasing structural role of moral capital in legitimizing institutional interpretation under compounded conditions. It is not equivalent to ethical leadership, mission clarity, or principled governance.

This chapter classifies moral credentialing as a structural failure mode for analytic purposes. It does not constitute institutional diagnosis, nor does it prescribe mission revision, reputational management strategy, or ethical oversight reform. The presence of articulated moral commitments does not imply dysfunction; moral credentialing becomes analytically significant only when compounded with additional structural preconditions.

Moral credentialing allows institutions to draw legitimacy from their perceived ethical commitments. When organizations accumulate reputational signals of virtue through mission statements, professional identities, or public narratives of service these signals can begin to shape how their actions are interpreted. Conducts that might otherwise invite scrutiny may instead be viewed through the presumption of benevolent intent.

Over time, this moral framing can influence not only how institutions are perceived but also how they communicate. As reputational legitimacy becomes tied to ethical identity, organizations increasingly rely on language that reinforces those associations. Statements emphasizing care, support, empowerment, healing, or guidance become central features of institutional messaging.

This language can serve important and genuine purposes. Many institutions do in fact pursue missions rooted in care and social responsibility. Yet when moral credentials are firmly established, the language associated with those credentials may also begin to function defensively. Expressions of care and ethical commitment can shape interpretation in ways that soften critique, redirect attention, or preempt deeper examination of institutional practices.

In this way, the moral legitimacy accumulated through credentialing often becomes embedded in communication itself. Language that signals benevolence, compassion, or service may begin to operate as a form of insulation, influencing how actions are perceived before their consequences are fully examined.

The following chapter explores this pattern of care-language shielding, examining how institutions oriented toward care and guidance may rely on morally resonant language that both affirms their mission and, under certain conditions, shields organizational practices from sustained scrutiny.

CHAPTER 13

CARE-LANGUAGE SHIELDING

Care-language shielding refers to the structural use of care-oriented terminology in ways that shape interpretive boundaries and may attenuate institutional recalibration under compounded structural conditions. It describes a semantic dynamic in which language associated with support, well-being, protection, or healing becomes increasingly central to institutional self-description and legitimacy framing.

This analysis does not evaluate the legitimacy of care professions, trauma-informed practice, compassionate institutional design, or service-oriented missions. The concept does not evaluate the ethical validity of care-centered institutional missions. Institutions that prioritize care, safety, and well-being perform essential social functions. The analytic concern is not the presence of care language, but the structural role such language may assume within interpretive and authority systems under attenuated corrective conditions.

Whereas moral credentialing concerns the consolidation of moral legitimacy capital, care-language shielding concerns the interpretive effects of care-centered semantic framing. It operates at the level of linguistic structure rather than moral standing.

Within Occupational Psychosis, care-language shielding is analyzed as a compounded semantic manifestation of authority consolidation under attenuated feedback conditions. It functions as an observable failure mode that may emerge when narrative capture, authority inflation, incentivized conformity, symbolic compliance, and moral credentialing converge. It does not imply insincerity, exaggeration, or ideological positioning. It describes a structural narrowing of interpretive permeability mediated through semantic emphasis.

Institutions frequently adopt care-oriented language to articulate commitment to safety, dignity, inclusion, and well-being. Such language may appear in mission statements, policy frameworks, strategic communications, and professional training materials. Under stable conditions, care language can enhance trust, signal responsibility, and reinforce ethical orientation.

Care-language shielding becomes analytically significant when care-oriented terminology begins to function as an interpretive stabilizer rather than solely as descriptive articulation.

Under compounded structural conditions, institutional actors may interpret critique through the lens of perceived misalignment with care commitments. Operational concerns may be reframed as threats to safety, inclusion, or well-being frameworks. Language associated with protection or harm prevention may become central to interpretive evaluation of dissenting input.

This dynamic does not require deliberate deflection. It may arise through sincere prioritization of care values. However, when care language becomes tightly integrated with authority validation and narrative coherence, recalibration thresholds may rise.

Care-language shielding thus describes a structural shift in which semantic framing contributes to reduced permeability between corrective input and institutional response.

Interaction With Other Modes

Care-language shielding frequently interacts with moral credentialing and narrative capture.

Moral positioning may reinforce care-centered self-description. Narrative capture may integrate care identity into institutional coherence. Incentivized conformity may reduce willingness to articulate concerns framed as potentially misaligned with care commitments. Symbolic compliance may demonstrate visible adherence to care protocols. Feedback suppression may attenuate signals that are linguistically reframed as destabilizing to protective environments.

Authority inflation may further consolidate interpretive centrality around care-oriented framing when leadership becomes the primary interpreter of safety or protection standards.

These interactions do not imply that care values are misapplied. Rather, they describe how semantic emphasis may structurally narrow interpretive flexibility under compounded preconditions.

Boundary Clarification

Care-language shielding does not imply that care professions, trauma-informed practices, or well-being initiatives are inherently distortive. Nor does it suggest that attention to psychological safety or inclusion undermines institutional integrity. The analytic concern arises only when semantic framing becomes structurally entangled with authority consolidation and reduced corrective permeability. The phenomenon concerns structural linguistic mediation, not moral orientation or professional legitimacy.

Within Occupational Psychosis, care-language shielding refers specifically to the increased structural influence of care-oriented terminology in shaping interpretive thresholds under compounded conditions. It is not equivalent to compassionate leadership, ethical service delivery, or protective governance.

This chapter classifies care-language shielding as a structural failure mode for analytic purposes. It does not constitute institutional diagnosis, nor does it prescribe revision of care terminology, psychological safety models, or trauma-informed frameworks. The presence of care-oriented language does not imply dysfunction; care-language shielding becomes analytically significant only when compounded with additional structural preconditions.

Care-language shielding illustrates how institutional communication can shape perception before actions are fully evaluated. When organizations emphasize language associated with compassion, service, or ethical responsibility, this framing can influence how observers interpret institutional behavior. Practices that might otherwise raise concern may be softened by narratives that highlight intention, mission, or commitment to care.

Over time, however, the protective effects of such language can have broader consequences. When critical feedback is filtered through moral framing and institutions continue to affirm their benevolent purpose, the signals that normally indicate institutional distress may lose their urgency. Patterns of strain, conflict, or dysfunction can begin to appear less exceptional and more routine.

This gradual shift alters how organizations and their members respond to emerging problems. Conditions that once might have triggered immediate corrective action may instead be interpreted as temporary difficulties, inevitable pressures, or the unavoidable costs of pursuing an important mission. The language of care, resilience, or dedication can reframe persistent institutional challenges as evidence of commitment rather than signals of systemic misalignment.

As a result, organizational crises may become absorbed into the everyday functioning of the system. What was once recognized as a warning signal can come to be treated as a normal feature of institutional life.

The following chapter examines this process of crisis normalization, exploring how repeated exposure to unresolved institutional strain can gradually recalibrate expectations until conditions that should prompt reform are instead accepted as routine.

CHAPTER 14

CRISIS NORMALIZATION

Crisis normalization refers to the progressive recalibration of institutional baseline expectations when temporary, exceptional, or strain conditions become structurally incorporated into routine operations. It describes a temporal shift in which measures, interpretations, or tolerances initially framed as provisional gradually assume durable status within institutional practice.

This analysis does not evaluate specific historical events, policy responses, or sectoral crises. Nor does it evaluate the appropriateness of emergency authorities or contingency governance mechanisms. The concept concerns structural temporal dynamics within institutional systems rather than commentary on particular episodes.

Within the framework of Occupational Psychosis, crisis normalization is analyzed as temporal threshold drift within institutional operating baselines rather than as a theory of sovereign exceptionalism. It functions as an observable failure mode that may emerge when authority inflation, feedback attenuation, narrative capture, and incentivized conformity converge under sustained strain. The concept does not presume intentional extension of emergency conditions or deliberate opportunism.

Institutions must adapt to disruption. The analytic concern arises when adaptive measures lose their provisional character without corresponding recalibration of baseline assumptions.

Crisis normalization operates at the level of threshold adjustment rather than interpretive coherence or legitimacy consolidation. It concerns what becomes considered ordinary.

Institutions routinely confront periods of disruption in resource scarcity, operational volatility, reputational strain, or environmental uncertainty. In response, provisional adjustments may be introduced to stabilize performance and maintain continuity. These adjustments may include modified procedures, temporary reporting standards, expedited decision pathways, or redefined performance thresholds.

Under ordinary conditions, provisional measures are time-bound and subject to periodic reassessment. Crisis normalization becomes analytically significant when temporary recalibrations persist beyond the initial strain context and gradually redefine baseline expectations.

Repeated invocation of exceptional framing may shift tolerance thresholds. Performance standards initially regarded as emergency accommodations may become embedded in routine evaluation. Heightened decision centralization may persist after immediate strain subsides. Documentation or reporting modifications may assume durable form.

This shift need not involve explicit declaration. Baseline recalibration may occur incrementally through cumulative extension of provisional practices. Crisis normalization thus describes a structural incorporation of exception into routine.

Interaction With Other Modes

Crisis normalization frequently interacts with authority inflation and narrative capture.

During strain periods, authority centralization may be justified as a stabilizing measure. If crisis framing persists, authority inflation may consolidate. Narrative capture may integrate exceptional conditions into institutional self-understanding. Incentivized conformity may reduce contestation of provisional measures framed as protective or necessary. Feedback suppression may attenuate signals questioning continued emergency status.

Symbolic compliance may demonstrate visible adherence to revised procedures, reinforcing their permanence. Care-language shielding may linguistically frame extended provisional measures as protective rather than transitional.

These interactions do not imply improper response to strain. Rather, they describe how temporal extension of provisional adaptation may alter institutional baselines under compounded preconditions.

Boundary Clarification

Crisis normalization does not imply that institutions should avoid emergency adaptation. Adaptive flexibility is necessary for resilience. Nor does it imply that temporary measures are inherently distortive.

The analytic concern arises only when provisional adjustments become structurally embedded without explicit recalibration of original baseline standards.

Within Occupational Psychosis, crisis normalization refers specifically to temporal threshold drift under sustained strain conditions. It is not equivalent to responsible contingency planning, resilience strategy, or adaptive governance.

This chapter classifies crisis normalization as a structural failure mode for analytic purposes. It does not constitute institutional diagnosis, nor does it prescribe reversal of emergency measures, policy redesign, or governance restructuring. The presence of adaptive response to disruption does not imply dysfunction; crisis normalization becomes analytically significant only when compounded with additional structural preconditions.

Crisis normalization alters the threshold at which institutions recognize conditions as exceptional or concerning. When persistent strain, conflict, or dysfunction becomes integrated into everyday operations, the signals that would ordinarily prompt corrective action lose their urgency. What was once understood as a deviation from healthy functioning gradually becomes accepted as a routine feature of institutional life.

Over time, this recalibration of expectations can affect more than organizational awareness of crisis. As systems adapt to persistent instability, the informal and formal boundaries that guide professional conduct may also begin to shift. Practices that were once constrained by clear role definitions, ethical standards, or accountability mechanisms can become increasingly flexible as institutions prioritize continuity and stability under pressure.

This process often unfolds gradually. Under conditions of normalized strain, individuals and organizations may begin to justify expanded roles, improvised responsibilities, or blurred lines of authority as necessary responses to ongoing challenges. Actions that would once have required careful deliberation may instead be interpreted as pragmatic adjustments within a system already accustomed to operating under stress.

In this way, the normalization of crisis can quietly erode the boundaries that help maintain institutional integrity. Distinctions between roles, responsibilities, and professional limits may become less defined as systems adapt to sustained instability.

The following, and final chapter, in Part II, examines this process of boundary erosion, exploring how prolonged exposure to normalized crisis conditions can weaken the structural and ethical limits that ordinarily regulate institutional authority and professional conduct.

CHAPTER 15

BOUNDARY EROSION

Boundary erosion refers to the gradual reduction in clarity of institutional role, scope, or functional differentiation under compounded structural conditions. It describes a shift in which the demarcations that ordinarily define institutional jurisdiction, responsibility, and authority become progressively less distinct.

This analysis does not imply institutional collapse, systemic failure, or organizational breakdown. Nor does it evaluate jurisdictional legitimacy, statutory authority, or institutional expansion strategy. Institutions frequently evolve, adapt, and expand in response to changing environments. The concept does not presume systemic instability or structural breakdown. The analytic concern arises only when structural differentiation becomes increasingly diffuse without corresponding recalibration of mandate or oversight.

Whereas authority inflation concerns amplification of interpretive centrality, and crisis normalization concerns temporal recalibration of baseline expectations, boundary erosion concerns lateral expansion and role indistinctness. It operates along the axis of scope rather than authority or time.

Within the framework of Occupational Psychosis, boundary erosion is analyzed as scope diffusion under attenuated corrective permeability rather than as a general theory of mission creep. It functions as an observable failure mode that may emerge when authority consolidation, feedback attenuation, incentivized conformity, symbolic compliance, moral credentialing, and crisis normalization converge. It does not presume overreach, misconduct, or strategic expansion. Rather, it describes structural diffusion under compounded preconditions.

Structural Emergence

Institutions are defined by boundaries. Mandates, professional standards, jurisdictional limits, and role differentiation establish predictable scope. These boundaries enable accountability, coordination, and public trust. Boundary erosion becomes analytically significant when scope expands incrementally without explicit structural clarification.

Under compounded conditions, interpretive centralization may increase authority over adjacent domains. Crisis adaptation may extend provisional functions beyond their initial temporal frame. Moral legitimacy consolidation may support broadened self-understanding of institutional mission. Care-language framing may expand protective or supportive interpretations of institutional responsibility.

Such expansion may occur gradually. New functions may be integrated without formal redefinition of mandate. Oversight distinctions may soften as role boundaries overlap. Functional differentiation between departments, professions, or governance bodies may narrow.

This process need not be deliberate. It may arise through cumulative accommodation to strain, ambiguity, or mission ambition. However, when boundary clarity diminishes without structural recalibration, accountability pathways may become less distinct. Boundary erosion thus describes progressive diffusion of institutional scope under compounded structural conditions.

Interaction With Other Modes

Boundary erosion frequently interacts with authority inflation and crisis normalization.

As authority centrality consolidates, interpretive jurisdiction may broaden. When provisional measures become routine, functional adjustments may persist beyond original constraints. Incentivized conformity may reduce internal contestation of expanding scope. Symbolic compliance may provide visible affirmation of newly integrated functions. Feedback suppression may attenuate signals that question mandate clarity.

Moral credentialing may reinforce broadened mission interpretation through accumulated legitimacy capital. Care-language shielding may linguistically frame expanded scope as protective or responsive.

These interactions do not imply that institutional evolution is inappropriate. Rather, they describe how cumulative structural shifts may soften demarcation clarity under attenuated corrective permeability.

Boundary Clarification

Boundary erosion does not imply that institutions should remain static or resist adaptation. Evolution of mandate can be legitimate and necessary. Nor does it suggest that functional overlap is inherently problematic.

The analytic concern arises only when expansion of scope occurs without corresponding structural clarification, recalibration of oversight, or reaffirmation of defined limits.

Within Occupational Psychosis, boundary erosion refers specifically to diminished clarity of role differentiation under compounded structural conditions. It is not equivalent to growth, diversification, or strategic development.

This chapter classifies boundary erosion as a structural failure mode for analytic purposes. It does not constitute institutional diagnosis, nor does it prescribe contraction of scope, jurisdictional redesign, or governance restructuring.

The presence of institutional adaptation does not imply dysfunction; boundary erosion becomes analytically significant only when compounded with additional structural preconditions.

Taxonomic Boundary Statement

The preceding chapters have classified a series of institutional failure modes associated with Occupational Psychosis. The institutional failure modes of epistemic narrowing, feedback suppression, incentivized conformity, symbolic compliance, authority inflation, moral credentialing, care-language shielding, crisis normalization, and boundary erosion are presented as analytic constructs rather than diagnostic determinations.

The taxonomy is descriptive, not prescriptive. It identifies structural patterns that may emerge under compounded preconditions of identity-role fusion, feedback attenuation, interpretive consolidation, and incentive distortion. The presence of any individual mode does not imply institutional dysfunction, ethical failure, or systemic instability.

The failure modes described in Part II are neither inevitable nor universal. Institutions may exhibit elements of these dynamics without experiencing distortion. The analytic framework does not presume linear progression, cumulative inevitability, or collapse. Nor does it assign causal primacy to any single condition.

This taxonomy does not establish measurement instruments, evaluative criteria, intervention protocols, or governance reforms. It does not authorize institutional diagnosis. Questions of application, operational assessment, certification, or structural redesign remain outside the scope of this volume.

The purpose of Part II is classification clarity. By differentiating vertical, temporal, semantic, and lateral structural dynamics, the taxonomy establishes conceptual boundaries necessary for disciplined analysis. It does not prescribe corrective action.

With the structural patterns identified, the analysis may now turn to a distinct question: under what conditions might early indicators of compounded structural drift become observable without collapsing descriptive taxonomy into premature evaluation? Part III, Systemic Drift Dynamics, proceeds under continued analytic restraint.

PART III

SYSTEMIC DRIFT DYNAMICS

CHAPTER 16

GRADUALISM AND NORMALIZATION OF DEVIATION

The indicators described in this section are conceptual in nature. They do not constitute measurement instruments, diagnostic criteria, or evaluative tools.

Gradualism and normalization of deviation refer to the incremental adjustment of institutional standards, expectations, or practices in ways that progressively redefine acceptable variance from established baselines. The concept describes a structural process through which small departures from original norms become incorporated into routine operations without explicit reauthorization.

This analysis does not imply negligence, safety failure, regulatory violation, professional malpractice, or systemic collapse. Institutions routinely adjust to operational realities. Nor does this analysis evaluate regulatory adequacy or institutional compliance regimes. The analytic concern arises only when incremental deviation accumulates without deliberate recalibration of original performance assumptions.

Within the framework of Occupational Psychosis, normalization of deviation is analyzed as a cross-domain structural drift mechanism rather than as a sector-specific safety phenomenon. Gradualism functions as a drift dynamic rather than a discrete failure mode. It explains how structural preconditions and failure patterns described in Parts I and II may stabilize over time without abrupt disruption. The concept concerns cumulative micro-adjustment rather than dramatic change.

Structural Mechanism

Institutions operate within defined performance parameters, professional standards, and procedural expectations. When minor deviations occur, they may initially be treated as situational adaptations, temporary accommodations, or contextual allowances.

If such deviations recur, tolerance thresholds may subtly adjust. What was once considered outside standard practice may gradually be reinterpreted as acceptable variance. Over time, deviation may cease to be recognized as deviation.

This process need not involve explicit policy revision. It may occur through tacit accommodation, resource constraint, interpretive reframing, or cultural adaptation. Gradualism thus describes incremental recalibration of institutional baselines without overt acknowledgment of change.

Interaction With Structural Preconditions

Gradualism interacts closely with feedback attenuation and authority insulation.

If corrective signals are dampened, small deviations may not trigger recalibration. If authority centrality is consolidated, reinterpretation of deviation may occur without distributed contestation. Narrative coherence may integrate adaptation into institutional identity. Incentivized conformity may discourage articulation of concern over incremental shifts.

The mechanism is cumulative rather than episodic. Normalization of deviation may therefore serve as a stabilizing pathway through which compounded structural dynamics persist without crisis or overt breakdown.

Distinction From Crisis Normalization

Crisis normalization (Chapter 14) concerns the incorporation of exceptional or emergency conditions into routine practice. Gradualism and normalization of deviation differ in that they do not require crisis framing. Drift may occur in stable environments through repeated accommodation to minor variances.

Crisis normalization is temporal incorporation of exception. Gradualism is incremental recalibration of tolerance. The former may arise during sustained strain. The latter may arise in ordinary operational continuity.

Boundary Clarification

Gradual adaptation is not inherently distortive. Institutions must evolve in response to complexity. The analytic concern arises only when cumulative micro-adjustments obscure the relationship between current practice and original standards without deliberate review.

Within Occupational Psychosis, gradualism is analyzed as a structural drift mechanism that may facilitate stabilization of failure modes under attenuated corrective permeability. It is not equivalent to innovation, adaptive learning, compliance erosion, or strategic refinement.

This chapter describes a structural mechanism of incremental drift. It does not authorize retrospective evaluation, performance audit, regulatory critique, or corrective intervention. The presence of incremental adjustment does not imply dysfunction; gradualism becomes analytically relevant only when compounded with additional structural preconditions.

Gradualism and the normalization of deviation illustrate how institutional systems can slowly recalibrate their expectations of acceptable conduct. When small departures from established standards occur repeatedly without meaningful correction, they begin to lose their status as deviations. Over time, practices that once appeared unusual or concerning become absorbed into routine operations.

As these shifts accumulate, responsibility for recognizing and addressing misalignment becomes increasingly difficult to locate. Because change occurs incrementally, no single moment appears sufficiently significant to trigger corrective intervention. Each step seems minor when viewed in isolation, even as the cumulative effect gradually alters the institutional landscape.

Under these conditions, accountability can become diffuse. Individuals operating within the system may perceive the emerging conditions as the product of broader institutional dynamics rather than the result of identifiable decisions or actions. Responsibility appears distributed across procedures, roles, and historical developments rather than concentrated in any one actor or moment of choice.

This diffusion of accountability represents an important continuation of the dynamics described in the preceding chapter. As deviations become normalized through gradual adjustment, the institutional capacity to attribute responsibility for those conditions may weaken.

The following chapter examines this process of diffusion of responsibility, exploring how institutional structures can disperse accountability across actors and processes in ways that make corrective action increasingly difficult to initiate.

CHAPTER 17

DIFFUSION OF RESPONSIBILITY

Diffusion of responsibility refers to the structural dispersion of corrective accountability across institutional layers in ways that may attenuate clarity of decision ownership under compounded conditions. It describes a dynamic in which responsibility for evaluation, recalibration, or corrective action becomes distributed across multiple actors or procedural channels without a clearly identifiable locus of decisive authority.

The concept does not imply intentional evasion, misconduct, abdication of duty, or ethical failure. The dynamic concerns structural dispersion, not individual avoidance of accountability. In complex institutions, responsibility is often shared across teams, committees, governance layers, and professional roles. Distributed responsibility can enhance deliberation and reduce unilateral error. The analytic concern arises only when dispersion of accountability reduces clarity regarding who holds final responsibility for corrective inflection.

Within Occupational Psychosis, diffusion of responsibility is analyzed at the institutional-structural level rather than as an individual psychological phenomenon. It functions as a systemic drift dynamic rather than a discrete failure mode. It explains how gradual deviation (Chapter 16) may persist without overt challenge when corrective ownership becomes structurally diffuse.

Diffusion concerns accountability clarity, not scope expansion. Unlike boundary erosion (Chapter 15), which addresses mandate diffusion, diffusion of responsibility addresses attenuation of corrective locus within existing scope.

Structural Mechanism

Institutions commonly rely on layered governance structures. Responsibilities may be divided among departments, committees, oversight bodies, and executive roles. Procedural safeguards may require consensus, review, or multi-stage authorization before decisions are finalized.

Under stable conditions, such distribution supports balanced deliberation. However, under compounded structural preconditions that include authority centralization, incentivized conformity, feedback attenuation, or narrative consolidation, corrective responsibility may become less clearly localized.

Concerns may be acknowledged but deferred to adjacent units. Evaluative responsibility may be distributed across committees without clear inflection authority. Procedural routing may create extended pathways between signal recognition and decisive response.

Over time, corrective clarity may soften. Responsibility may be shared broadly without a singular actor holding unambiguous authority to initiate recalibration. This process need not involve conscious avoidance. It may arise from structural complexity, layered review processes, or cultural emphasis on collective governance. Diffusion thus describes attenuation of corrective ownership rather than absence of responsibility.

Interaction With Drift Dynamics

Diffusion of responsibility interacts closely with gradualism (Chapter 16). When incremental deviations accumulate, corrective intervention often requires a clear locus of authority. If responsibility for recognizing or acting upon deviation is structurally diffuse, micro-adjustments may continue without decisive recalibration. Diffusion also interacts with reputation preservation cycles (Chapter 18), as shared responsibility may distribute reputational exposure across actors, reducing individual impetus for corrective inflection.

Authority inflation may paradoxically coexist with diffusion. While interpretive centrality consolidates upward, operational accountability for micro-level correction may remain dispersed. This asymmetry may reduce clarity regarding where recalibration authority resides. The mechanism is subtle. It concerns structural dispersion, not individual intent.

Distinction From Boundary Erosion

Boundary erosion concerns diffusion of institutional scope or mandate. Diffusion of responsibility concerns dispersion of corrective accountability within established scope.

An institution may maintain clearly defined jurisdiction while still exhibiting attenuated clarity regarding who is responsible for responding to deviation. Conversely, scope may expand without diffused accountability if corrective authority remains centralized.

The two dynamics are analytically distinct, though they may interact under compounded conditions.

Boundary Clarification

Diffusion of responsibility does not imply that shared governance is inherently problematic. Distributed accountability can enhance deliberation and institutional resilience. Nor does it evaluate bureaucratic efficiency, organizational hierarchy, or governance model selection.

The analytic concern arises only when dispersion of responsibility attenuates clarity of corrective authority under structural preconditions that already reduce feedback permeability.

Within Occupational Psychosis, diffusion of responsibility refers specifically to diminished clarity of corrective locus in complex institutional systems. It is not equivalent to collaboration, interdisciplinary governance, or participatory leadership.

This chapter describes a structural dynamic of accountability dispersion. It does not authorize attribution of fault, retrospective evaluation of specific institutions, or prescriptive redesign of governance structures. The presence of shared responsibility does not imply dysfunction; diffusion becomes analytically relevant only when compounded with additional structural conditions described in prior chapters.

Diffusion of responsibility illustrates how institutional accountability can become distributed across roles, procedures, and historical developments in ways that make corrective action increasingly difficult to initiate. When responsibility appears widely dispersed, no single actor or decision point carries clear ownership for addressing emerging misalignment. Institutional conditions may therefore persist not because they are actively defended, but because responsibility for confronting them is unclear.

Yet this diffusion rarely operates in isolation. Even in systems where accountability is broadly dispersed, institutions remain attentive to how they are perceived by external audiences and internal stakeholders. Organizational survival, legitimacy, and authority are often closely tied to the preservation of reputation.

Under such conditions, institutional responses to emerging concerns may begin to prioritize the protection of credibility and trust. Actions taken to address criticism, manage public perception, or reassure stakeholders can become organized around maintaining reputational stability rather than examining underlying conditions. As responsibility becomes diffuse, reputational considerations may increasingly shape how problems are interpreted and how responses are structured.

Over time, this dynamic can give rise to repeating patterns of response. Institutions confronted with criticism or concern may adopt measures designed to restore confidence, signal accountability, or reaffirm commitment to institutional values. While such responses may provide short-term stabilization, they can also reinforce cycles in which reputational repair takes precedence over deeper structural correction.

The following chapter examines these reputation preservation cycles, exploring how institutions may repeatedly engage in actions aimed at maintaining legitimacy and credibility even as the underlying conditions generating concern remain unresolved.

CHAPTER 18

REPUTATION PRESERVATION CYCLES

Reputation preservation cycles refer to recurrent institutional patterns in which internal recalibration is moderated by perceived risks to external legitimacy, continuity, and stakeholder confidence. The concept describes structural feedback loops through which concerns about reputational stability influence the pace, scope, or visibility of corrective adjustment.

The concept does not imply deception, concealment, strategic misrepresentation, or prioritization of image over substance. The dynamic concerns structural stabilization, not reputational manipulation. Institutions depend upon external trust to function. Reputation is not merely symbolic; it supports funding, authority, participation, professional standing, and public legitimacy. Attention to reputational continuity is therefore structurally rational.

Within the framework of Occupational Psychosis, reputation preservation cycles are analyzed as structural recalibration moderators under attenuated corrective permeability rather than as communication strategy frameworks. They function as systemic drift dynamics rather than failure modes. They explain how corrective recalibration may become moderated when reputational equilibrium is perceived as fragile. The analytic concern is structural moderation of adjustment under compounded conditions, not ethical misconduct.

Reputation preservation concerns dynamic equilibrium, not moral positioning. Unlike moral credentialing (Chapter 12) which concerns accumulated legitimacy capital, reputation preservation cycles concern ongoing stabilization of perceived institutional continuity.

Structural Mechanism

Institutions operate within ecosystems of stakeholders, regulators, professionals, beneficiaries, and public observers. External confidence influences institutional survival and resource stability. As a result, reputational signals often receive sustained attention within governance structures.

Under stable conditions, reputational awareness coexists with internal recalibration. However, under compounded structural preconditions that include authority consolidation, diffusion of responsibility, feedback attenuation, or narrative rigidity reputational considerations may increasingly shape how corrective signals are processed.

Concerns may be evaluated not solely on substantive merit but also in relation to perceived impact on institutional continuity. Corrective measures may be paced to reduce volatility or preserve stakeholder confidence. Recalibration may be structured in ways that maintain stability during adjustment.

This dynamic does not evaluate transparency norms, media engagement practices, or stakeholder communication models. It may arise through structural prioritization of continuity in complex environments where abrupt change is perceived as destabilizing. Over time, reputational equilibrium may become a moderating variable in corrective decision-making.

Cyclical Reinforcement

Reputation preservation becomes cyclical when stabilization reinforces the perception that equilibrium must be maintained. If moderated recalibration successfully preserves confidence, institutional actors may infer that gradual adjustment is preferable to abrupt inflection.

Under such conditions, incremental correction may be favored over structural revision. Feedback signals may be incorporated in ways that maintain continuity while limiting perceived disruption.

This cycle does not imply resistance to improvement. Rather, it describes a structural pattern in which preservation of institutional continuity interacts with other drift dynamics to shape the tempo of recalibration. Reputation thus functions as both stabilizer and moderator.

Interaction With Drift Dynamics

Reputation preservation cycles interact closely with diffusion of responsibility (Chapter 17) and gradualism (Chapter 16). When corrective ownership is diffuse, reputational risk may be distributed across actors, reducing impetus for decisive inflection. Incremental adjustment may align with perceived reputational safety. Narrative coherence may integrate moderate recalibration into existing institutional identity.

Authority inflation may reinforce reputational stabilization if interpretive centrality shapes how reputational risk is assessed. Moral credentialing may further strengthen external legitimacy, increasing institutional confidence in maintaining continuity. These interactions do not imply that institutions privilege appearance over substance. They describe how reputational equilibrium can structurally moderate recalibration under attenuated corrective permeability.

Distinction From Moral Credentialing

Moral credentialing concerns accumulation and invocation of ethical legitimacy capital.

Reputation preservation cycles concern dynamic moderation of institutional recalibration within external legitimacy ecosystems. An institution may maintain stable reputation without invoking moral standing. Conversely, moral credentialing may occur without active reputational moderation cycles.

The two dynamics are analytically distinct, though they may interact.

Boundary Clarification

Reputation preservation does not imply concealment, image manipulation, or strategic misrepresentation. Nor does it suggest that institutions should disregard external confidence. Stable reputation is essential for institutional functioning. The analytic concern arises only when reputational equilibrium structurally moderates corrective recalibration under compounded preconditions.

Within Occupational Psychosis, reputation preservation cycles refer specifically to recurrent stabilization dynamics that may influence tempo and visibility of adjustment. They are not equivalent to public relations practice, stakeholder engagement, or communication management.

This chapter describes a structural stabilization dynamic. It does not authorize retrospective judgment, reputational audit, communication reform, or prescriptive governance redesign. The presence of reputational consideration does not imply dysfunction; reputation preservation becomes analytically relevant only when compounded with additional structural conditions described in prior chapters. The dynamics described here remain analytic classifications intended to clarify institutional patterns associated with Occupational Psychosis rather than determinations regarding specific individuals, organizations, or professions.

Reputation preservation cycles stabilize institutional standing by reinforcing continuity of interpretation and minimizing visible disruption. Over time, however, the effects of this stabilization extend beyond organizational signaling and begin to shape the internal commitments of those operating within the system. As reputational coherence is maintained, alignment with prevailing narratives becomes increasingly tied to professional standing, credibility, and belonging. It is within this progression that reputation management gives way to a more durable condition. The next chapter examines how professional identity may become progressively anchored to the system it sustains, narrowing the range of positions that can be held without personal or professional consequence.

CHAPTER 19

PROFESSIONAL IDENTITY LOCK-IN

Professional identity lock-in refers to the progressive stabilization and rigidity of collective professional self-definition under compounded structural conditions. It describes a dynamic in which established norms, interpretive frameworks, role expectations, and professional standards become increasingly resistant to revision over time.

The concept does not imply incompetence, resistance to learning, professional inadequacy, or ethical deficiency. It does not evaluate professional legitimacy, credential integrity, or the social value of specialized expertise. Professions require stability of identity to maintain expertise, public trust, and coherent standards of practice. Professional continuity is essential for institutional reliability and knowledge transmission. The analytic concern arises only when collective identity stabilization becomes structurally rigid under conditions that already attenuate corrective permeability.

Within the framework of Occupational Psychosis, professional identity lock-in is analyzed as a compounded rigidity dynamic under attenuated corrective permeability rather than as a theory of professional closure or monopolization. It functions as a systemic drift dynamic rather than a structural precondition. Unlike identity-role fusion (Chapter 2), which concerns individual-level integration of self and occupational role, professional identity lock-in concerns collective rigidity in professional self-definition across institutional settings. Lock-in addresses systemic persistence rather than psychological attachment.

Structural Mechanism

Professions develop through shared training pathways, credentialing systems, ethical codes, and disciplinary norms. Over time, interpretive coherence strengthens collective identity. Standards become codified. Norms become institutionalized. Boundary definitions clarify scope and jurisdiction.

Under stable conditions, such coherence supports excellence and accountability. However, under compounded structural preconditions that include authority consolidation, reputational stabilization, diffusion of responsibility, and gradual tolerance drift professional identity may become less flexible in response to novel information or environmental complexity.

Revisions to role interpretation may require negotiation across credentialing bodies, institutional leadership, and peer communities. Established frameworks may be reinforced through training, evaluation metrics, and cultural transmission. Interpretive alternatives may be considered but incorporated gradually.

This process does not imply stagnation. Professions routinely evolve. The analytic relevance arises only when collective identity stabilization interacts with other drift dynamics to reduce adaptive responsiveness.

Professional identity lock-in thus describes rigidity of collective interpretive self-definition under attenuated corrective permeability.

Interaction With Drift Dynamics

Professional identity lock-in interacts closely with reputation preservation cycles (Chapter 18). Stable professional identity supports reputational continuity. In turn, reputational equilibrium may reinforce established identity frameworks.

Gradualism (Chapter 16) may normalize incremental adaptation within existing identity boundaries rather than prompt structural redefinition. Diffusion of responsibility (Chapter 17) may distribute accountability for revising professional standards across multiple actors, reducing clarity of locus for identity recalibration.

Authority inflation may reinforce dominant professional interpretations, particularly when leadership positions are occupied by individuals strongly embedded within prevailing identity frameworks.

The dynamic is cumulative. Identity stability may gradually shift toward rigidity when corrective signals are moderated across multiple structural channels.

Distinction From Identity-Role Fusion

Identity-role fusion concerns psychological integration between individual self-concept and occupational role. Professional identity lock-in concerns collective stabilization of professional self-definition at the institutional level.

An individual may exhibit identity-role fusion without systemic lock-in. Collective identity rigidity may persist even when individual professionals remain reflective and adaptable. The two constructs are analytically distinct but may interact under compounded conditions.

Boundary Clarification

Professional identity lock-in does not suggest that professions resist reform, suppress innovation, or disregard evidence. Nor does it assess regulatory authority, disciplinary governance structures, or institutional autonomy.

The analytic concern arises only when collective identity stabilization reduces flexibility in interpreting new information or recalibrating standards under structural preconditions that already attenuate feedback.

Within Occupational Psychosis, professional identity lock-in refers specifically to rigidity in collective interpretive self-definition under compounded structural conditions. It is not equivalent to expertise, specialization, credentialing integrity, professional autonomy, or regulatory governance.

This chapter describes a structural dynamic of identity stabilization and potential rigidity. It does not authorize critique of specific professions, disciplinary bodies, credentialing institutions, or regulatory frameworks. It does not prescribe reform of professional standards or educational models. The presence of stable professional identity does not imply dysfunction; lock-in becomes analytically relevant only when compounded with additional structural conditions described in prior chapters.

Professional identity lock-in illustrates how occupational roles can become deeply integrated with individual and institutional identity. When professional legitimacy, personal credibility, and organizational purpose converge around a shared identity narrative, the capacity for reflexive reassessment may gradually narrow. Questioning institutional practices can begin to feel indistinguishable from questioning the identity of the profession itself.

Over time, this dynamic can shape how authority operates within the system. When professional identity becomes closely tied to institutional legitimacy, those occupying positions of authority may draw credibility not only from their formal roles but also from the collective identity of the profession they represent. Institutional narratives and professional identity reinforce one another, stabilizing perceptions of legitimacy and expertise.

Under these conditions, authority may become increasingly insulated from corrective pressures. Signals that challenge prevailing interpretations can be filtered through professional identity commitments, while institutional structures continue to affirm the authority of those already positioned to define acceptable practice. The result is a system in which authority and identity mutually reinforce one another.

This dynamic introduces the next pattern of institutional reinforcement. When professional identity lock-in converges with institutional authority structures, the system can begin to generate self-reinforcing authority loops in which legitimacy, authority, and institutional narratives continually validate one another.

The following chapter examines self-reinforcing authority loops, exploring how institutional systems can stabilize authority through feedback processes that make external correction increasingly difficult to initiate.

CHAPTER 20

SELF-REINFORCING AUTHORITY LOOPS

Self-reinforcing authority loops refer to recursive feedback dynamics in which institutional interpretations are validated and stabilized through processes that preferentially reproduce existing authority structures. The concept describes cyclical mechanisms through which authority-generated interpretations shape institutional responses, and those responses in turn reinforce the interpretive centrality of authority.

The concept does not imply authoritarian intent, suppression of dissent, improper consolidation of power, or illegitimate governance. It does not assess democratic versus centralized governance models. Authority is a necessary feature of coordinated institutional action. The analytic concern arises only when feedback dynamics disproportionately confirm existing interpretive frameworks under compounded structural conditions.

Within the framework of Occupational Psychosis, self-reinforcing authority loops are analyzed as compounded recursive stabilization dynamics under attenuated corrective permeability rather than as general feedback theory or political power analysis. They function as systemic drift dynamics rather than structural preconditions or discrete failure modes. Unlike authority inflation (Chapter 11), which concerns amplification of interpretive centrality, self-reinforcing loops concern recursive validation processes that stabilize authority over time. The emphasis is dynamic rather than positional.

Structural Mechanism

Institutions rely on feedback systems to evaluate performance, interpret outcomes, and guide recalibration. Authority structures often serve as central nodes within these evaluative processes. Decisions flow downward; performance data and reporting flow upward; interpretations are synthesized and redistributed.

Under stable conditions, feedback systems integrate diverse signals and permit recalibration. However, under compounded structural preconditions that include diffusion of responsibility, reputation preservation cycles, professional identity lock-in, and gradual tolerance drift feedback pathways may increasingly route through authority-centered interpretive frames.

Interpretive outcomes may confirm prior assumptions. Performance measures may be constructed or weighted in ways consistent with prevailing authority narratives. Corrective signals may be incorporated incrementally rather than prompting structural revision.

Over time, authority interpretations may become self-validating. Decisions produce outcomes interpreted through existing frameworks; those interpretations reinforce the authority that articulated them.

Recursive validation may arise from structural complexity, institutional habit, or procedural design rather than from deliberate control of information flows.

Self-reinforcing authority loops thus describe cyclical stabilization of interpretive centrality through feedback recursion.

Recursive Dynamics

Authority loops operate through repetition rather than escalation. Each cycle of decision, outcome interpretation, and redistribution of authority framing reinforces prior assumptions.

Feedback channels may remain formally intact while becoming structurally aligned with prevailing interpretations. Evaluation criteria may evolve in ways that reflect dominant frameworks. Reporting structures may prioritize information congruent with established direction.

The system appears stable because it is coherent. Coherence, however, may increasingly reflect internal validation rather than external variance integration.

This process does not require suppression of dissent. It may occur even in institutions that formally encourage dialogue. The critical variable is the weighting and integration of feedback within authority-centered interpretive nodes.

Interaction With Drift Dynamics

Self-reinforcing authority loops interact closely with prior drift dynamics in Part III.

Gradualism (Chapter 16) may normalize small deviations that align with authority interpretation. Diffusion of responsibility (Chapter 17) may attenuate clarity regarding who can challenge recursive patterns. Reputation preservation cycles (Chapter 18) may moderate recalibration in ways that reinforce continuity. Professional identity lock-in (Chapter 19) may stabilize interpretive frameworks that authority embodies.

Authority inflation (Chapter 11) increases the likelihood that loops become durable. However, recursive stabilization can occur even in distributed systems if interpretive weighting converges around dominant nodes. The interaction is systemic rather than hierarchical.

Distinction From Authority Inflation

Authority inflation concerns the concentration and amplification of interpretive centrality. Self-reinforcing authority loops concern the recursive reproduction of that centrality through feedback cycles. Inflation describes a structural configuration. Loops describe a dynamic stabilization process.

An institution may exhibit authority inflation without fully recursive validation loops if corrective permeability remains high. Conversely, recursive loops may operate in systems with moderate authority concentration if feedback integration is disproportionately aligned with dominant interpretations. The two constructs are analytically distinct but structurally interactive.

Boundary Clarification

Self-reinforcing authority loops do not imply illegitimate governance, political authoritarianism, or intentional suppression of critique. Nor do they evaluate leadership effectiveness, strategic coherence, regulatory authority, or institutional hierarchy.

The analytic concern arises only when recursive validation reduces adaptive responsiveness under compounded structural conditions. Within Occupational Psychosis, self-reinforcing authority loops refer specifically to feedback recursion that stabilizes interpretive dominance under attenuated corrective permeability. They are not equivalent to centralized governance, disciplined execution, or institutional coordination.

This chapter describes a recursive systems dynamic. It does not authorize critique of specific leaders, governance structures, or institutional hierarchies. It does not prescribe decentralization, restructuring, or procedural redesign. The presence of coherent authority systems does not imply dysfunction; self-reinforcing loops become analytically relevant only when compounded with additional structural conditions described in prior chapters.

The preceding chapters have examined a series of institutional dynamics through which occupational systems may gradually lose alignment with corrective feedback and external reality. When these dynamics converge epistemic narrowing, feedback suppression, incentivized conformity, symbolic compliance, authority inflation, and the reinforcing processes that follow, they can generate institutional environments in which authority becomes increasingly self-validating. Self-reinforcing authority loops represent the culmination of these interacting conditions, stabilizing systems that are progressively less responsive to signals of misalignment.

Yet even within such environments, signals of institutional strain rarely disappear entirely. Concerns, anomalies, and early indicators of misalignment often continue to emerge within different parts of the system. The challenge is that these signals do not always travel intact. As information moves through organizational layers, it may be filtered, reframed, softened, or delayed before reaching positions capable of initiating corrective action.

Understanding these patterns requires shifting the analytic lens. The preceding chapters have focused primarily on the structural conditions through which institutional distortion becomes stabilized. The next section turns to the early warning indications that may appear within systems experiencing these conditions. Rather than examining how distortion is maintained, this section explores how signals of emerging misalignment are generated, transmitted, and interpreted within hierarchical organizations.

The first of these indicators concerns the way institutional signals change as they move across organizational layers. Communication originating from operational levels may gradually lose clarity, urgency, or meaning as it travels upward through administrative structures. By the time it reaches decision-making authority, the original signal may be significantly altered.

The following chapter examines early warning indicators and signal attenuation across hierarchical layers, exploring how institutional communication can transform as it moves through organizational structures and how these transformations can obscure early indications of systemic strain.

PART IV

EARLY WARNING INDICATORS

CHAPTER 21

SIGNAL ATTENUATION ACROSS HIERARCHICAL LAYERS

The indicators described in this section are conceptual in nature. They do not constitute measurement instruments, diagnostic criteria, evaluative tools, or operational frameworks. They are descriptive structural signal patterns that may warrant reflective inquiry under compounded institutional distortion.

Signal attenuation across hierarchical layers refers to the gradual weakening, transformation, or reduction in contrast of evaluative information as it moves through institutional levels. It describes a structural pattern in which signals generated at one layer are progressively reframed, summarized, or integrated as they pass across reporting, supervisory, and interpretive boundaries.

The concept does not imply intentional suppression, censorship, misrepresentation, or improper control of information. Informational transformation across levels is a routine feature of institutional complexity. In layered systems, translation and summarization are necessary for coordination. Attenuation may therefore arise from structural mediation rather than from deliberate distortion.

Within the framework of Occupational Psychosis, signal attenuation is analyzed as a perceptual surface indicator emerging from compounded drift dynamics rather than as a theory of communication failure. It functions as a descriptive observation of informational contrast under attenuated corrective permeability. It does not assess transparency norms, reporting integrity, or compliance practices. Signal attenuation concerns informational transformation under structural complexity.

Hierarchical institutions depend upon layered communication pathways. Data may originate from operational environments, service interfaces, or frontline interactions. As information moves upward, it may be categorized, aggregated, or reframed to align with reporting standards and strategic synthesis requirements.

Similarly, interpretive direction may move downward through strategic narratives, policy articulation, or performance guidance. Translation occurs in each direction.

Under stable conditions, such translation enhances coherence and reduces noise. However, under compounded structural dynamics, including diffusion of responsibility, reputation preservation cycles, professional identity lock-in, and self-reinforcing authority loops, feedback transmission may gradually narrow in contrast.

Signals that diverge from prevailing interpretive frames may be incorporated incrementally within existing categories. Ambiguity may be resolved through alignment with established narratives. Variance may be represented in aggregate form rather than contextual detail. This process may occur through routine standardization and procedural normalization. Signal attenuation thus describes reduced amplitude or altered clarity of feedback across hierarchical layers.

Interaction With Drift Dynamics

Signal attenuation interacts with prior dynamics that are described in Parts II and III.

Gradualism may reduce perceptual contrast of incremental deviation. Diffusion of responsibility may disperse ownership of signal interpretation. Reputation preservation cycles may influence the framing of potentially destabilizing information. Professional identity lock-in may shape the interpretive categories through which signals are understood. Self-reinforcing authority loops may weight feedback in ways that reinforce prevailing frameworks. Under such conditions, feedback may remain present yet exhibit reduced differentiation. Signal attenuation therefore functions as a descriptive surface manifestation of compounded structural processes rather than as evidence of communicative breakdown.

Descriptive Characteristics

Signal attenuation does not present as the absence of information. Institutions may continue to generate reports, summaries, performance updates, and strategic communications. Formal channels may remain intact.

The perceptual shift occurs in relative contrast. Variance may appear less differentiated across levels. Corrective impulses may appear less pronounced. Interpretive alignment may appear smoother between hierarchical strata. This pattern may reflect increased coherence. It may also reflect progressive narrowing of informational amplitude. The analytic relevance arises only when attenuation coincides with drift dynamics described in earlier sections.

Boundary Clarification

Signal attenuation across hierarchical layers does not imply that hierarchical structures are inherently distortive. Layered communication is essential for institutional coordination and governance. Nor does the concept evaluate leadership intent, transparency standards, regulatory reporting, or institutional compliance frameworks.

Within Occupational Psychosis, signal attenuation refers specifically to descriptive changes in feedback contrast under compounded structural conditions. It does not constitute a measurement instrument, performance audit, or diagnostic framework. It is an interpretive observation, not an evaluative judgment.

This chapter identifies a conceptual indicator of informational transformation across institutional layers. It does not authorize investigation, attribution of responsibility, communication redesign, or structural intervention. The presence of layered translation does not imply dysfunction; attenuation becomes analytically relevant only when interpreted in conjunction with the structural dynamics described in Parts II and III.

CHAPTER 22

RECALIBRATION DELAY UNDER NON-CRISIS CONDITIONS

Recalibration delay under non-crisis conditions refers to the gradual extension of time between the emergence of evaluative signals and substantive institutional adjustment in environments not characterized by acute disruption. It describes a structural pattern in which adaptive revision unfolds more slowly when deviation accumulates incrementally rather than through visible crisis.

The concept does not imply negligence, indifference, incompetence, or institutional avoidance. Nor does it evaluate administrative efficiency, decisional agility, or governance effectiveness. Institutions frequently prioritize stability in the absence of acute threat. Non-crisis environments often favor continuity, predictability, and procedural regularity. Deliberation, consultation, and staged revision are common features of responsible governance.

Within the framework of Occupational Psychosis, recalibration delay is analyzed as a temporal moderation pattern emerging from compounded drift dynamics rather than as a theory of organizational inertia or resistance to change. It reflects how systemic stabilization mechanisms may influence the tempo of institutional adjustment when deviation unfolds gradually. Temporal extension of adaptive cycles may reflect prudence, deliberation, or institutional care rather than distortion. Recalibration delay concerns pacing, not absence of responsiveness.

Structural Conditions

Institutional recalibration typically involves interpretive reassessment, procedural modification, and communicative alignment. These processes require coordination across professional, managerial, and governance layers.

Under stable conditions, such pacing ensures coherence and reduces volatility. However, when drift unfolds incrementally through gradualism, diffusion of responsibility, reputation preservation cycles, professional identity lock-in, and recursive authority reinforcement recalibration may be temporally moderated.

In the absence of visible crisis markers, signals may not generate urgency thresholds. Deviations may be interpreted as manageable variance rather than structural shift. Interpretive continuity may be maintained while adjustment is phased or extended across deliberative cycles.

This temporal extension does not imply resistance to change. It reflects a structural orientation toward stability in non-emergency contexts. Recalibration delay thus describes elongation of adaptive cycles under conditions of incremental variance.

Interaction With Drift Dynamics

Recalibration delay interacts closely with gradualism (Chapter 16). When deviation occurs incrementally, urgency signals may remain muted. Diffusion of responsibility, (Chapter 17), may distribute ownership of corrective timing. Reputation preservation cycles, (Chapter 18), may moderate visible inflection. Professional identity lock-in (Chapter 19), may frame deviation within established interpretive boundaries. Self-reinforcing authority loops (Chapter 20) may stabilize prevailing interpretations during extended reassessment periods.

These interactions may increase the temporal distance between signal recognition and structural recalibration. Recalibration delay therefore functions as a descriptive temporal manifestation of compounded structural moderation rather than as evidence of institutional deficiency.

Descriptive Characteristics

Recalibration delay does not present as inactivity. Institutions may continue to deliberate, review, communicate, and refine incrementally. Policy statements may acknowledge evolving conditions. Adjustments may occur in stages rather than through abrupt revision. The perceptual pattern emerges when adaptation unfolds more slowly relative to the pace of incremental variance.

In non-crisis contexts, the absence of visible inflection points may reinforce perceptions of continuity. Stability may be interpreted as adequacy. Incremental accommodation may replace comprehensive reassessment. The analytic relevance arises only when temporal moderation coincides with the drift dynamics described in earlier sections.

Distinction From Crisis Normalization

Crisis normalization, (Chapter 14), concerns incorporation of sustained strain into routine practice. Recalibration delay under non-crisis conditions differs in that it occurs without acute disruption. It reflects temporal moderation of adjustment during incremental drift rather than adaptation to sustained emergency. Crisis normalization is shaped by overload. Recalibration delay is shaped by stability. The two are structurally distinct though potentially interactive.

Boundary Clarification

Recalibration delay does not assess compliance timeliness, legal obligation, operational throughput, or administrative competence. It does not imply that rapid adjustment is inherently preferable to measured deliberation. Institutions frequently balance responsiveness with continuity. Extended evaluation may reflect prudence rather than distortion.

Within Occupational Psychosis, recalibration delay refers specifically to temporal extension of adaptive cycles under compounded drift conditions. It is a descriptive indicator, not a diagnostic threshold or performance metric.

This chapter identifies a conceptual pattern of temporal moderation in institutional adjustment. It does not authorize performance benchmarking, regulatory critique, decisional audit, or prescriptive reform. The presence of measured pacing does not imply dysfunction; recalibration delay becomes analytically relevant only when interpreted in conjunction with the structural dynamics described in Parts II and III.

CHAPTER 23

NARRATIVE OVER-INTEGRATION OF CORRECTIVE FEEDBACK

Narrative over-integration of corrective feedback refers to a structural pattern in which evaluative signals are incorporated into prevailing institutional narratives in ways that preserve coherence without substantially altering interpretive frameworks. It describes a dynamic through which feedback is acknowledged and absorbed, yet primarily within existing meaning structures.

The concept does not imply deception, manipulation, strategic reframing, or rhetorical misrepresentation. Institutions rely on narrative coherence to maintain continuity, shared identity, and strategic direction. Integrating feedback into established narratives can support stability and reduce fragmentation. Interpretive integration may reflect institutional efforts toward coherence rather than the avoidance of substantive reconsideration. The analytic concern arises only when integration becomes so seamless that it reduces the disruptive potential of corrective signals.

Within the framework of Occupational Psychosis, narrative over-integration is analyzed as an interpretive stabilization pattern under attenuated corrective permeability rather than as a theory of storytelling or rhetorical strategy. It does not evaluate political communication, media engagement, public persuasion practices, or public relations management. It reflects how interpretive systems may adapt to feedback while preserving underlying structural assumptions. The emphasis is on interpretive absorption rather than narrative distortion.

Structural Mechanism

Institutions articulate guiding narratives to orient action and maintain shared understanding. These narratives may include mission articulation, strategic priorities, professional commitments, or value frameworks. Corrective feedback typically enters these interpretive systems through reporting channels, evaluations, stakeholder input, or performance review processes.

Under stable conditions, feedback may prompt refinement or recalibration of narrative framing. However, under compounded structural dynamics that include gradualism, diffusion of responsibility, reputation preservation cycles, professional identity lock-in, and recursive authority reinforcement, corrective signals may be integrated in ways that reaffirm prevailing interpretive structures.

Feedback may be acknowledged within the language of existing commitments. Adjustments may be framed as extensions of established direction rather than as departures from it. Variance may be positioned as confirmation of adaptive capacity rather than as indication of structural reconsideration.

This process need not involve resistance to change. It may arise from the structural function of narrative in preserving institutional coherence across complexity. Narrative over-integration thus describes interpretive absorption that preserves continuity while moderating transformative recalibration.

Interaction With Drift Dynamics

Narrative over-integration interacts closely with reputation preservation cycles (Chapter 18) and self-reinforcing authority loops (Chapter 20). Stable narratives support reputational continuity and may reinforce authority-centered interpretation.

Gradualism (Chapter 16) may allow incremental deviation to be integrated narratively without visible rupture. Diffusion of responsibility (Chapter 17) may diffuse ownership of narrative revision. Professional identity lock-in (Chapter 19) may stabilize interpretive categories within which feedback is framed.

Under such conditions, feedback may be present, acknowledged, and incorporated while interpretive continuity remains largely intact. Narrative over-integration therefore functions as a descriptive surface manifestation of interpretive stabilization under compounded structural conditions.

Descriptive Characteristics

Narrative over-integration does not present as silence, denial, or concealment. Institutions may openly reference feedback, acknowledge complexity, and affirm commitment to learning and improvement. Language may emphasize responsiveness and adaptation.

The perceptual shift occurs when incorporation of feedback consistently reinforces existing interpretive frameworks rather than prompting structural reconsideration.

Corrective signals may be framed as validation of current direction. Variance may be interpreted as manageable refinement rather than as indication of deeper recalibration. The analytic relevance arises only when over-integration coincides with the structural dynamics described in Parts II and III.

Distinction From Reputation Preservation

Reputation preservation cycles (Chapter 18) concern moderation of recalibration to maintain external legitimacy. Narrative over-integration concerns internal interpretive absorption of feedback within prevailing meaning structures.

An institution may preserve reputation without over-integrating feedback. Conversely, narrative over-integration may occur in the absence of reputational pressure. The two dynamics are analytically distinct though potentially interactive.

Boundary Clarification

Narrative over-integration does not evaluate communication ethics, transparency standards, political discourse, or institutional persuasion practices. It does not imply that continuity of narrative is inherently distortive or that revision is inherently preferable.

Narrative coherence is necessary for coordination and shared meaning. The analytic concern arises only when interpretive absorption consistently moderates transformative recalibration under compounded structural conditions.

Within Occupational Psychosis, narrative over-integration refers specifically to descriptive patterns of feedback absorption within stabilized interpretive systems. It is not equivalent to strategic messaging, rhetorical manipulation, media framing, or public relations management.

This chapter identifies a conceptual pattern of interpretive stabilization. It does not authorize critique of specific communications, narrative frameworks, institutional statements, or public messaging practices. It does not prescribe narrative revision or structural reform. The presence of narrative coherence does not imply dysfunction; over-integration becomes analytically relevant only when interpreted in conjunction with the structural dynamics described in earlier sections.

As corrective signals become absorbed into prevailing narratives, their disruptive potential may be reduced without requiring corresponding structural adjustment. In such conditions, narrative coherence can be maintained even as underlying performance conditions shift. The next chapter examines how this dynamic may be accompanied by metric stability amid outcome variance, where measured indicators remain consistent despite changes in underlying realities.

CHAPTER 24

METRIC STABILITY AMID OUTCOME VARIANCE

Metric stability amid outcome variance refers to a structural pattern in which established performance measures remain relatively unchanged while contextual conditions or substantive outcomes exhibit incremental variation. It describes a perceptual dynamic in which continuity in metric reporting coexists with evolving operational realities.

The concept does not imply manipulation, misreporting, selective disclosure, or intentional distortion of data. It does not assess accounting integrity, financial disclosure practices, quantitative reporting validity, or compliance standards. Performance metrics are often designed to provide continuity across reporting periods and institutional cycles. Measurement continuity may reflect institutional commitment to comparability and longitudinal discipline rather than evaluative distortion.

Within the framework of Occupational Psychosis, metric stability amid outcome variance is analyzed as a contextual alignment pattern under compounded drift dynamics rather than as a critique of performance measurement systems. It reflects how measurement continuity may interact with incremental contextual change when interpretive recalibration unfolds gradually. The emphasis is on structural alignment between evaluative architecture and evolving environment.

Structural Conditions

Institutions rely on metrics to coordinate action, evaluate progress, and communicate performance. Measurement frameworks frequently remain stable over time to preserve comparability and reduce volatility in reporting.

Under stable environmental conditions, such continuity supports clarity and coherence. However, when operational context evolves incrementally through shifts in demand, stakeholder expectations, technological change, or resource configuration, the established metrics may not immediately adjust.

Under compounded structural dynamics that include gradualism, diffusion of responsibility, reputation preservation cycles, professional identity lock-in, and self-reinforcing authority loops, measurement systems may retain continuity even as contextual variance accumulates.

Outcomes may exhibit gradual divergence from initial assumptions while metric structures remain constant. Reporting may continue to demonstrate internal coherence and stability. This pattern does not imply that metrics are inaccurate or invalid. It describes temporal asynchrony between evolving context and measurement recalibration. Metric stability thus reflects structural continuity in evaluation frameworks amid gradual environmental change.

Interaction With Drift Dynamics

Metric stability amid outcome variance interacts with narrative over-integration (Chapter 23) and recalibration delay (Chapter 22). Stable metrics may reinforce narrative continuity and moderate urgency for structural reassessment.

Gradualism (Chapter 16) may normalize incremental outcome shifts without prompting metric revision. Diffusion of responsibility (Chapter 17) may distribute ownership of measurement recalibration. Reputation preservation cycles (Chapter 18) may favor continuity in performance representation. Professional identity lock-in (Chapter 19) may stabilize interpretive categories embedded in measurement systems. Self-reinforcing authority loops (Chapter 20) may weight metrics aligned with prevailing interpretive frames.

Under such conditions, measurement continuity and contextual variance may coexist without visible rupture. The analytic relevance arises only when this coexistence aligns with compounded structural dynamics.

Descriptive Characteristics

Metric stability amid outcome variance does not present as reporting breakdown. Institutions may continue to publish structured evaluations, performance summaries, and strategic indicators. Measures may remain internally consistent and methodologically coherent.

The perceptual shift occurs when contextual change becomes more pronounced than metric evolution. Measurement categories may remain stable while underlying conditions shift incrementally. Indicators may reflect continuity even as environmental complexity increases. Adjustment may occur within existing metric parameters rather than through structural reconsideration of measurement design.

This pattern may reflect prudence, comparability discipline, and institutional coherence. It may also reflect delayed alignment between evolving context and evaluative architecture. The analytic concern arises only when persistent asynchrony coincides with the drift dynamics described in earlier sections.

Distinction From Metric Inflation

Metric inflation (Chapter 4) concerns expansion, substitution, or proliferation of indicators in ways that alter interpretive clarity. Metric stability amid outcome variance differs in that measurement frameworks remain stable rather than expanding or substituting. The dynamic here concerns continuity of evaluative structure despite contextual evolution. The two constructs are analytically distinct though potentially interactive.

Boundary Clarification

Metric stability amid outcome variance does not evaluate data accuracy, financial reporting ethics, regulatory disclosure practices, or performance management legitimacy. It does not imply that metrics should be frequently revised or that stability is undesirable.

Measurement continuity is often necessary for longitudinal comparison and institutional coherence. The analytic concern arises only when measurement stability coincides with incremental contextual divergence under compounded structural conditions.

Within Occupational Psychosis, this construct refers specifically to descriptive alignment patterns between evaluative frameworks and evolving environments. It is not a diagnostic instrument, audit protocol, or performance assessment model.

This chapter identifies a conceptual indicator of temporal alignment between measurement systems and contextual evolution. It does not authorize auditing, benchmarking, financial review, or reform of performance metrics. The presence of stable metrics does not imply dysfunction; analytic relevance emerges only when interpreted in conjunction with the structural dynamics described in Parts II and III.

When measured indicators remain stable despite shifts in underlying conditions, attention may increasingly rely on the interpretation of those indicators rather than their correspondence to operational reality. In such environments, shared interpretive frames can consolidate, narrowing the range of plausible readings. The next chapter examines how this process may lead to interpretive convergence without contestability.

CHAPTER 25

INTERPRETIVE CONVERGENCE WITHOUT CONTESTABILITY

Interpretive convergence without contestability refers to a structural pattern in which institutional interpretations become increasingly aligned across hierarchical and professional levels while opportunities for meaningful alternative framing gradually narrow. It describes a perceptual condition in which consensus appears stable and internally coherent, yet interpretive plurality becomes less visible within formal decision environments.

The concept does not imply censorship, suppression of dissent, ideological conformity, or intentional exclusion of alternative views. Institutions require shared interpretive alignment to coordinate action. Interpretive convergence may reflect successful coordination, professional coherence, or effective communication. The analytic concern arises only when convergence coincides with reduced structural contestability under compounded drift conditions.

Within the framework of Occupational Psychosis, interpretive convergence without contestability is analyzed as a structural alignment pattern under attenuated corrective permeability rather than as a theory of groupthink or ideological conformity. It does not evaluate deliberative norms, constitutional design, governance models, political discourse, or institutional openness to disagreement. It concerns interpretive structure, not ideological orientation. The emphasis is on narrowing interpretive variance rather than on restriction of expression.

Structural Conditions

Institutional coherence depends upon shared frameworks. Strategic direction, professional standards, and operational priorities require alignment across levels. Over time, interpretive categories may stabilize through training, reporting structures, leadership articulation, and cultural reinforcement.

Under stable conditions, convergence enhances clarity and coordination. However, when gradualism, diffusion of responsibility, reputation preservation cycles, professional identity lock-in, and recursive authority reinforcement operate in combination, interpretive diversity may narrow in subtle ways.

Alternative frames may continue to exist but may be integrated within dominant narratives before generating substantive reconsideration. Interpretive deviation may appear increasingly rare within formal deliberative spaces. Discussion may exhibit high internal coherence across levels and roles.

This process does not require overt policy constraint or attitudinal rigidity. It may arise through structural reinforcement of prevailing categories and the natural human preference for cognitive consistency.

Interpretive convergence thus describes increasing alignment; contestability concerns the structural availability of meaningful alternative framing within decision environments.

Interaction With Drift Dynamics

Interpretive convergence interacts closely with narrative over-integration (Chapter 23) and self-reinforcing authority loops (Chapter 20). Stable narratives and recursive validation may reinforce interpretive coherence across levels.

Gradualism (Chapter 16) may reduce perceptual contrast of incremental divergence. Diffusion of responsibility (Chapter 17) may diffuse ownership of interpretive challenge. Reputation preservation cycles (Chapter 18) may moderate the visibility of alternative framing. Professional identity lock-in (Chapter 19) may stabilize shared interpretive assumptions.

Under such compounded conditions, interpretive convergence may appear as stability rather than narrowing. The analytic relevance arises when convergence aligns with attenuated corrective permeability.

Descriptive Characteristics

Interpretive convergence without contestability does not present as absence of dialogue. Institutions may continue to hold meetings, publish position statements, and conduct structured deliberation. Participation mechanisms may remain formally intact.

The perceptual shift occurs in the relative scarcity of sustained alternative framing within formal interpretive spaces. Consensus may appear rapid and internally consistent. Variance may be reframed within prevailing categories rather than generating structural reconsideration. Interpretive alignment may extend across levels without visible inflection points.

This pattern may reflect institutional maturity, clarity, and coherence. It may also reflect cumulative stabilization of dominant interpretive structures. The analytic concern arises only when convergence coincides with other drift dynamics described in earlier sections.

Distinction From Declining Dissent Tolerance

Declining dissent tolerance would concern explicit reduction in openness to disagreement. Interpretive convergence without contestability differs in that formal tolerance may remain intact while structural availability of alternative framing narrows through cumulative alignment. The dynamic concerns interpretive architecture rather than attitudinal stance. The two constructs are analytically distinct though potentially interactive.

Boundary Clarification

Interpretive convergence without contestability does not evaluate freedom of expression, civil discourse norms, constitutional protections, regulatory governance, or political ideology. It does not imply that consensus is inherently distortive or that pluralism is inherently superior.

Institutions often require interpretive convergence to function effectively. The analytic concern arises only when convergence aligns with attenuated corrective permeability under compounded structural conditions.

Within Occupational Psychosis, this construct refers specifically to descriptive patterns of interpretive alignment within institutional decision systems. It is not a diagnostic criterion, governance audit, or ideological critique.

This chapter identifies a conceptual indicator of interpretive alignment under structural stabilization. It does not authorize evaluation of specific deliberative processes, institutional cultures, governance models, or political frameworks. The presence of consensus does not imply dysfunction; interpretive convergence becomes analytically relevant only when interpreted in conjunction with the structural dynamics described in Parts II and III.

Interpretive convergence without contestability marks a stage in which institutional actors increasingly rely on the same explanatory language and interpretive assumptions. Alternative perspectives may still exist, but they rarely gain traction within the dominant frame.

Yet convergence of interpretation does not mean institutional language becomes fixed. Organizations often continue to adjust their vocabulary, adopting new terms that signal responsiveness to emerging concerns or criticism. The appearance of linguistic adaptation can suggest learning or reform, even when underlying structures remain largely unchanged. The following chapter examines this condition more closely, focusing on how institutions may adopt adaptive language without corresponding structural shift.

CHAPTER 26

ADAPTIVE LANGUAGE WITHOUT STRUCTURAL SHIFT

Institutions rarely remain linguistically static when confronted with criticism, emerging knowledge, or shifting public expectations. Organizational vocabulary evolves continuously as leaders respond to internal concerns, regulatory pressures, and broader cultural change. New terminology appears in mission statements, policy documents, training materials, and public communications. Concepts such as accountability, transparency, inclusion, well-being, and innovation enter institutional discourse and are repeated across formal and informal channels.

At first glance, these linguistic adaptations may appear to signal meaningful organizational learning. The adoption of new language often conveys responsiveness and suggests that institutions are integrating corrective feedback. However, the presence of updated terminology does not necessarily indicate that underlying structures, incentives, or authority relationships have been altered.

Adaptive language without structural shift occurs when institutional vocabulary evolves while the operational configuration of the system remains largely unchanged. In these cases, the organization becomes increasingly fluent in the language of reform, yet the mechanisms through which decisions are made, feedback is processed, and accountability is enforced continue to operate as they did previously.

Several conditions contribute to this pattern. External scrutiny may create pressure to demonstrate awareness of emerging issues. Professional communities may introduce new normative language that signals legitimacy within a field. Leadership teams may also adopt updated terminology as a way of maintaining alignment with prevailing expectations without undertaking disruptive structural change.

Over time, this linguistic adaptation can produce a subtle but important form of institutional stabilization. The organization appears to be responding to criticism, learning from experience, and incorporating new perspectives. Yet because structural arrangements remain intact, the underlying dynamics that generated earlier problems may persist.

From an observational standpoint, adaptive language without structural shift functions as an early warning indicator rather than definitive evidence of institutional failure. Language change can certainly accompany genuine reform. The indicator becomes meaningful only when evolving vocabulary is repeatedly unaccompanied by corresponding adjustments to governance, authority relationships, or decision processes.

Recognizing this distinction requires attention to the relationship between discourse and structure. When institutional language evolves but structural patterns remain stable, observers may be witnessing the emergence of a system that has become increasingly capable of absorbing critique without undergoing substantive recalibration.

The purpose of identifying this pattern is diagnostic rather than prescriptive. The discussion is intended to support institutional self-examination and scholarly analysis, not to provide strategies for narrative management or symbolic reform.

The indicators examined in this section identify patterns that may signal emerging institutional distortion. Yet the presence of early warning signals does not guarantee that observers will recognize them, nor that institutions will respond to them effectively. Signals can be overlooked, misinterpreted, or absorbed into existing narratives that preserve the appearance of stability.

Part V turns to the limits of detection. It examines why early warning indicators frequently fail to trigger meaningful correction, how institutional environments shape what can be recognized as a problem, and why systems may continue to appear functional even as distortion becomes increasingly embedded.

PART V

LIMITS OF DETECTION

LIMITS OF DETECTION

The indicators described in Part IV are conceptual surface manifestations of deeper structural dynamics. They are perceptual patterns that may appear when compounded preconditions and drift mechanisms interact over time. However, the presence or absence of such indicators does not conclusively establish the presence or absence of distortion.

Institutional systems are complex, adaptive, and often opaque. Feedback may be partial, mediated, or temporally lagged. Interpretive alignment may reflect health in one context and rigidity in another. Metric stability may signal coherence in one environment and asynchrony in another. For these reasons, early warning indicators must be interpreted with restraint.

Part V examines the epistemic constraints inherent in detecting systemic distortion. It explores why surface patterns may be ambiguous, why corrective permeability may fluctuate, and why well-designed evaluative systems encounter limits in identifying structural drift.

Detection is neither linear nor definitive. Understanding these limits is essential to preserving analytic integrity and preventing overextension of the framework.

CHAPTER 27

WHY INSTITUTIONAL ACTORS RARELY PERCEIVE DISTORTION

Institutional distortion, when it emerges, rarely presents itself as distortion to those operating within the system. This is not primarily a function of inattentiveness, indifference, or incompetence. Rather, it reflects the structural conditions under which institutional perception is formed, filtered, and stabilized.

Institutions are interpretive systems. They generate categories, standards, and evaluative frameworks through which information is understood. Actors within institutions operate through these shared structures of meaning. As a result, perception is mediated rather than direct.

Within the framework of Occupational Psychosis, perceptual limitation is analyzed as an emergent property of institutional structure rather than as a failure of awareness or attentional vigilance. The rarity of distortion recognition among institutional actors is therefore understood as structurally conditioned rather than personally deficient. The question is not why actors "miss" distortion, but how institutional interpretive architecture shapes what can be recognized as such. Perception is conditioned by structure.

Structural Mediation of Perception

Institutional actors rely on established interpretive categories to process information. Professional training, reporting structures, performance indicators, and governance frameworks provide coherence. These structures enable coordination but also stabilize perception.

Structural sociology has long recognized that organizations construct environments as much as they respond to them (Meyer & Rowan, 1977; March & Olsen, 1989). Meaning is institutionalized through routines and normative commitments. Actors interpret signals through categories that have been reinforced over time.

Under such conditions, incremental deviation may be integrated within existing interpretive frameworks rather than recognized as structural shift. Gradualism (Chapter 16) reduces perceptual contrast. Narrative over-integration (Chapter 23) stabilizes meaning. Metric continuity (Chapter 24) reinforces evaluative coherence. Interpretive convergence (Chapter 25) aligns perception across levels. Distortion, when present, may therefore appear as continuity. This is not concealment. It is structural mediation.

Institutional Systems Analysis

Institutions function as complex adaptive systems. Feedback flows through hierarchical layers (Chapter 21). Recalibration unfolds through deliberative pacing (Chapter 22). Reputation preservation cycles (Chapter 18) moderate interpretive inflection. Professional identity lock-in (Chapter 19) stabilizes role-based meaning structures.

These dynamics create systemic reinforcement loops that privilege coherence over disruption. Organizational learning literature demonstrates that actors often interpret anomalies within existing models before revising core assumptions (Argyris & Schön, 1978). Sensemaking processes prioritize plausibility over accuracy under conditions of complexity (Weick, 1995). Distortion may therefore remain structurally normalized within interpretive frames that continue to appear rational and internally consistent. The rarity of recognition reflects bounded rationality and institutional embeddedness rather than personal deficiency (Simon, 1947; March, 1994).

Governance Implications

From a governance perspective, perception is distributed rather than centralized. Boards, executives, professionals, and stakeholders operate within differentiated informational domains. Authority structures are designed to stabilize action, not to generate constant structural self-suspicion.

Institutional actors must balance vigilance with continuity. Excessive destabilization undermines coordination; insufficient recalibration risks drift. Governance design therefore moderates perception through formal procedures and legitimacy structures (Selznick, 1957; Luhmann, 1995).

Under compounded drift dynamics, the very mechanisms that preserve order may attenuate recognition of structural distortion. This does not indicate governance collapse. It reflects the inherent tension between stability and reflexivity in complex systems. Recognition is structurally constrained by the architecture of authority and meaning.

Epistemic Limitation

All institutional actors operate within interpretive horizons shaped by role, position, and embedded knowledge. Information asymmetry, hierarchical translation, and professional specialization fragment perception across domains.

External observers may perceive variance that internal actors normalize. Internal actors may perceive contextual nuance that external observers misinterpret. Neither vantage point provides complete visibility.

Distortion, when it accumulates gradually, may only become recognizable retrospectively, after thresholds have shifted or contextual rupture has occurred. The limits of perception are therefore structural and epistemic. They are not reducible to awareness alone.

Boundary Clarification

This chapter does not assert that institutional actors are incapable of recognizing distortion. Nor does it suggest inevitability of perceptual failure. Many institutions demonstrate adaptive reflexivity and corrective capacity.

The analytic claim is narrower in that recognition of distortion is structurally mediated by interpretive architecture, feedback design, governance pacing, and institutional embeddedness. Within Occupational Psychosis, the rarity of immediate distortion recognition reflects bounded perception under compounded structural conditions. It is not a moral judgment, a psychological diagnosis, or an indictment of institutional actors.

If distortion is rarely perceived directly, the question shifts from perception to correction. Even when variance becomes partially visible, structural forces may moderate internal adjustment or external accountability.

The following chapters examine how barriers to correction arise within institutional systems, how accountability is mediated across boundaries, and how early signals may carry asymmetrical cost. Detection is not merely perceptual. It is structurally conditioned.

CHAPTER 28

STRUCTURAL BARRIERS TO INTERNAL CORRECTION

Internal correction within institutional systems requires coordination across interpretive, procedural, and authority structures. When variance becomes partially visible, adjustment must be translated into policy reconsideration, metric recalibration, professional realignment, and communicative coherence. These processes are inherently complex.

Structural barriers to internal correction do not necessarily reflect resistance, unwillingness, or obstruction. Rather, they arise from the architectural features that enable institutions to function reliably under ordinary conditions. Stability, specialization, and distributed authority create resilience, but they also introduce friction into large-scale recalibration.

Within the framework of Occupational Psychosis, structural barriers are analyzed as coordination constraints within distributed authority systems rather than as expressions of resistance to reform. They are not interpreted as moral failures or intentional suppression of change. The focus is architectural, not accusatory. Correction is structurally mediated.

Coordination Complexity

Institutions operate through differentiated roles and layered decision pathways. Professional domains possess specialized knowledge; governance bodies maintain oversight; executive leadership integrates strategic direction. Adjustment within such systems requires alignment across these domains.

Institutional theory has long emphasized that formal structures are embedded within normative and cognitive frameworks (Meyer & Rowan, 1977; March & Olsen, 1989). Change must therefore traverse both procedural and interpretive layers. Organizational learning research demonstrates that modification of underlying assumptions is more demanding than adjustment of surface routines (Argyris & Schön, 1978).

When deviation accumulates gradually, the need for recalibration may not generate immediate structural consensus. Coordination demands time, negotiation, and interpretive alignment. Structural barriers thus often reflect the complexity of distributed decision-making rather than active opposition to change.

Role Differentiation and Responsibility Diffusion

Institutions distribute authority to maintain checks and balances. Boards govern, executives manage, professionals implement, and oversight bodies review. This distribution enhances accountability under stable conditions.

However, distributed authority also fragments responsibility for initiating correction. Diffusion of responsibility (Chapter 17) may create uncertainty regarding who possesses mandate to recalibrate foundational assumptions. Role clarity in routine operations does not always translate into clarity during structural reassessment.

Professional identity lock-in (Chapter 19) may further stabilize established practices, not through resistance, but through deeply embedded normative commitments. Correction therefore requires cross-boundary coordination that may not be immediately synchronized.

Procedural Stabilization

Formal procedures exist to reduce volatility. Policy revision processes, review cycles, and governance protocols provide structured pathways for change. These mechanisms protect institutions from abrupt or destabilizing shifts.

Under compounded drift dynamics, however, procedural pacing may moderate corrective velocity. Recalibration delay (Chapter 22) may interact with established review cycles, extending the timeline of adjustment. This pacing does not imply inaction. It reflects the structural design of institutions to privilege deliberation over rapid transformation. Structural barriers may therefore be experienced as friction rather than obstruction.

Legitimacy and Continuity

Institutions must maintain legitimacy with stakeholders, constituents, and governance authorities. Abrupt acknowledgment of foundational recalibration may introduce uncertainty. Reputation preservation cycles (Chapter 18) may therefore influence how and when correction is articulated.

Such moderation does not necessarily prevent adjustment; it may shape its sequencing. Internal correction often unfolds incrementally to preserve continuity and coherence. Stability and reflexivity exist in tension. Structural barriers emerge at the intersection of these imperatives.

Systemic Reinforcement

Complex adaptive systems exhibit self-reinforcing tendencies. Self-reinforcing authority loops (Chapter 20) may stabilize prevailing interpretations, particularly when metrics and narratives remain internally coherent (Chapters 23 and 24). Interpretive convergence (Chapter 25) may further align perception across levels.

Under such conditions, recalibration requires not only procedural change but interpretive shift. The greater the coherence of prevailing frameworks, the more demanding their revision becomes. This is not intentional entrenchment. It is structural reinforcement.

Boundary Clarification

Structural barriers to internal correction do not imply inevitability of stagnation. Many institutions successfully revise assumptions, recalibrate policies, and adapt to evolving environments.

The analytic claim is limited: correction within complex institutional systems is mediated by architectural features that introduce coordination friction. These features, which support reliability and legitimacy, may simultaneously moderate the speed or scope of adjustment under compounded drift dynamics.

Within Occupational Psychosis, structural barriers refer to system-level coordination constraints rather than to intentional obstruction, governance failure, or ethical deficiency.

If internal correction is structurally mediated, external accountability mechanisms may also encounter boundary constraints. Institutions do not operate in isolation; they are embedded within regulatory, cultural, and professional ecosystems.

The next chapter examines how external barriers to accountability is similarly shaped by structural mediation rather than by simple transparency or oversight deficits. Correction is neither automatic nor purely internal. It is systemically conditioned across boundaries.

CHAPTER 29

EXTERNAL BARRIERS TO ACCOUNTABILITY

Institutions operate within broader regulatory, professional, and cultural ecosystems. External accountability mechanisms interact with institutional systems through defined channels and jurisdictional boundaries whether formal oversight bodies, peer institutions, stakeholder networks, or public evaluative processes.

External barriers to accountability do not necessarily reflect evasion, resistance, or deliberate opacity. Rather, they arise from the structural differentiation between systems. Each institutional domain operates according to distinct mandates, informational architectures, and procedural logics. When distortion accumulates gradually within one system, external systems may encounter constraints in perceiving, interpreting, or responding to that accumulation.

Within the framework of Occupational Psychosis, external barriers are analyzed as inter-system translation constraints rather than as commentary on regulatory adequacy, political governance, or oversight sufficiency. The analytic focus remains structural, not accusatory. Accountability across boundaries is structurally mediated.

System Differentiation

Modern institutional environments are characterized by functional differentiation (Luhmann, 1995). Legal systems, professional associations, regulatory bodies, governance boards, and public constituencies operate under distinct decision logics. Information meaningful within one domain may not translate directly into another.

External oversight mechanisms rely on reporting protocols, jurisdictional authority, and defined evaluative criteria. When deviation unfolds incrementally within internal interpretive frames (Chapters 16-26), external systems may receive signals filtered through institutional mediation.

This filtering does not imply concealment. It reflects the structural necessity of translation across differentiated domains. External actors may therefore encounter partial visibility rather than comprehensive insight.

Jurisdictional Constraints

External accountability is often bounded by mandate. Oversight bodies typically review specific dimensions such as financial reporting, procedural compliance, professional standards, or regulatory adherence. These mandates rarely encompass the full interpretive architecture of institutional systems.

As a result, certain forms of gradual interpretive drift may not fall neatly within existing review categories. Metric stability (Chapter 24) may appear to be compliant. Narrative coherence (Chapter 23) may align with the stated mission. Interpretive convergence (Chapter 25) may appear as professional consensus.

When accountability frameworks are domain-specific, structural drift that spans domains may not be immediately legible within any single external jurisdiction. These limitations reflect mandate boundaries rather than oversight deficiency.

Information Asymmetry and Translation

External systems depend upon information provided through structured channels. Reporting cycles, audit frameworks, and compliance documentation translate internal operations into standardized forms. Information asymmetry is therefore structural. External observers receive representations designed for comparability and procedural clarity. Internal nuance may not be fully transmissible through these channels.

Organizational sociology has long noted that formal reporting can both illuminate and simplify complex realities (Meyer & Rowan, 1977; Power, 1997). Simplification supports governance but may attenuate contextual variance. External accountability systems operate within these translation constraints.

Temporal Misalignment

External oversight often functions on periodic cycles such as annual reviews, scheduled audits, and regulatory reporting intervals. Gradual deviation may accumulate between review cycles without triggering immediate recalibration.

Recalibration delay (Chapter 22) within internal systems may coincide with periodic oversight pacing. When both internal and external systems privilege continuity and procedural stability, incremental drift may not generate synchronized response.

This temporal misalignment does not imply absence of accountability. It reflects coordination limits across systems operating on different time scales.

Inter-System Legitimacy

External accountability mechanisms must themselves maintain legitimacy within their own domains. Oversight bodies balance enforcement with institutional stability. Excessive intervention may disrupt sector continuity; insufficient intervention may undermine credibility.

Thus, external systems operate within tension between vigilance and restraint. Accountability is negotiated within this tension rather than exercised in isolation.

External barriers to accountability therefore emerge at the intersection of differentiated mandates, translation constraints, temporal pacing, and legitimacy considerations. They are structural features of complex institutional ecosystems.

Boundary Clarification

External barriers to accountability do not imply that oversight is ineffective, that regulatory systems fail, or that institutions evade scrutiny. Many institutional ecosystems demonstrate robust accountability processes and adaptive recalibration.

The analytic claim is limited in that cross-boundary detection and correction of gradual distortion are mediated by jurisdictional differentiation, information translation, and temporal coordination constraints.

Within Occupational Psychosis, external barriers refer to inter-system structural limitations rather than to political critique, regulatory condemnation, or governance indictment.

If internal perception (Chapter 27), internal correction (Chapter 28), and external accountability (this chapter) are all structurally mediated, then early recognition of distortion may involve asymmetrical professional and social risk.

Signals that emerge before structural consensus forms may carry cost for those who articulate them. The following chapter examines how early dissent, when it arises within stabilized systems, can encounter structural risk asymmetries that shape institutional response. Detection is not only structurally constrained. It is also socially and professionally situated.

The preceding chapter examined how external accountability is mediated through institutional interfaces, periodic review cycles, and jurisdictional constraints. These structures can limit the timing, scope, and interpretation of corrective signals. Under certain conditions, external oversight remains present but becomes episodic, filtered, or decoupled from internal system dynamics. As a result, accountability may exist in form while operating with reduced capacity to generate sustained corrective adjustment.

The question that follows is not whether accountability mechanisms are present, but whether they retain sufficient structural alignment to influence system behavior. When internal constraints and external limitations converge, the conditions for correction may narrow further. In such configurations, corrective signals may continue to circulate but fail to produce meaningful revision. Chapter 30 examines these convergence conditions, focusing on the threshold at which correction becomes structurally constrained rather than procedurally unavailable.

CHAPTER 30

WHEN CORRECTION BECOMES STRUCTURALLY IMPOSSIBLE

Correction within institutional systems is ordinarily mediated rather than obstructed. As discussed in prior chapters, perception is structurally filtered, internal recalibration is coordinated across differentiated roles, and external accountability operates through jurisdictional translation. In most institutional environments, these mechanisms, though complex, permit adjustment over time.

Structural impossibility, as used here, refers to a theoretical limit condition within institutional architecture rather than to an empirical expectation, predictive claim, or generalizable outcome. Structural impossibility of correction represents a rare boundary condition. It does not describe routine friction, delay, or incremental stabilization. Rather, it refers to the convergence of compounded structural dynamics in such a way that corrective pathways become functionally inaccessible within the existing institutional architecture.

Within the framework of Occupational Psychosis, structural impossibility is analyzed as an extreme convergence case rather than as a claim of inevitability or universal outcome. It serves as a theoretical boundary model that clarifies the outer limits of institutional correction under specific compounded conditions. The emphasis is analytical, not predictive.

Convergence of Compounded Dynamics

Correction becomes structurally constrained when multiple drift dynamics align simultaneously. Interpretive convergence narrows the range of available reframing pathways, while metric stability can mask underlying contextual divergence. Narrative over-integration may absorb corrective signals before they prompt revision, and self-reinforcing authority loops can stabilize prevailing interpretations. At the same time, procedural pacing may extend recalibration cycles, reducing the system's responsiveness, while external oversight encounters limits in translating across jurisdictions. Together, these interacting conditions can restrict the capacity for meaningful correction even when signals remain present.

Individually, each dynamic is compatible with institutional stability. Collectively, under sustained alignment, they may create a closed interpretive system. This closure does not require intent, concealment, or active resistance. It emerges from recursive reinforcement across internal and external layers.

Structural sociology has long noted that institutions may become self-referential when interpretive coherence becomes highly stabilized (Luhmann, 1995). Organizational learning research suggests that double-loop revision becomes increasingly difficult when foundational assumptions are embedded within identity structures (Argyris & Schön, 1978).

Under rare conditions of cumulative reinforcement, corrective signals may circulate within existing frames without altering core architecture. This constitutes structural closure.

Theoretical Boundary Model

Structural impossibility should be understood as a boundary model rather than an empirical generalization. It clarifies what occurs when adaptive mechanisms that ordinarily preserve stability become mutually reinforcing in ways that reduce reflexive permeability.

The model is theoretical in that it represents a limiting case, does not imply frequency, does not predict trajectory, and does not assume permanence. Institutions may oscillate near such thresholds without crossing them. External shocks, leadership transitions, environmental shifts, or governance redesign may reopen corrective pathways.

The purpose of articulating this boundary is to define the structural conditions under which internal recalibration may become highly constrained, not to assert that institutions inevitably reach such a state.

Governance Breakdown Precursor

From a governance perspective, structural impossibility of correction signals a weakening of reflexive capacity. Governance systems rely on feedback loops capable of challenging foundational assumptions. When interpretive, procedural, and authority structures reinforce one another without permeability, governance becomes self-confirming rather than self-correcting.

This condition does not necessarily manifest as visible crisis. Institutions may appear coherent, stable, and procedurally compliant. Metrics may remain consistent; narratives may remain aligned; interpretive consensus may persist.

The breakdown is not operational but reflexive. Governance breakdown in this sense refers to the diminished capacity for structural self-examination. It is a precursor state, not a terminal condition. Without renewed permeability, accumulated divergence may only become visible through external rupture or environmental shock. Such rupture is not assumed. It is structurally possible.

Structural Lock-In and Identity

Professional identity lock-in (Chapter 19) plays a significant role in extreme convergence cases. When institutional identity becomes tightly fused with existing interpretive frameworks, revision may be experienced as existential destabilization rather than routine recalibration.

Institutions often define themselves through mission, values, and legacy commitments. Under high convergence conditions, identity defense may reinforce narrative absorption and metric continuity. This reinforcement is not inherently maladaptive; identity cohesion supports resilience. However, when cohesion interacts with attenuated corrective permeability, structural lock-in may occur. Lock-in is not synonymous with collapse. It is a condition of reduced adaptive bandwidth.

Rarity and Contingency

It is important to emphasize the rarity and contingency of structural impossibility. Most institutions retain multiple corrective channels and distributed reflexive capacity. The convergence described here requires sustained alignment of several dynamics without countervailing disruption.

Environmental complexity, stakeholder plurality, and leadership turnover frequently reintroduce interpretive diversity. External review cycles may reopen deliberation. Professional renewal may shift identity boundaries.

Structural impossibility is therefore best understood as a theoretical extreme, a boundary that clarifies limits rather than defines norms.

Boundary Clarification

This chapter does not assert that institutions inevitably entrench or that governance systems fail irreversibly. Nor does it imply that distortion, once stabilized, cannot be corrected. The analytic claim is narrower in that, under rare conditions of compounded convergence, corrective pathways may become functionally inaccessible within existing structural configurations.

Within Occupational Psychosis, structural impossibility serves as a conceptual boundary marker. It identifies the outer limit of reflexive constraint under compounded drift dynamics. It does not authorize prediction, diagnostic labeling, or evaluative judgment.

If structural impossibility represents the outer limit of institutional correction, then analytic humility becomes essential. Detection of such conditions is itself subject to perceptual mediation, jurisdictional constraint, and interpretive ambiguity.

The last chapter examines the epistemic boundary of institutional analysis. It clarifies why claims of distortion, impossibility, or breakdown must remain constrained by limits of inference, evidentiary ambiguity, and structural complexity.

CHAPTER 31

THE EPISTEMIC BOUNDARY OF INSTITUTIONAL ANALYSIS

Institutional analysis operates within epistemic limits. Complex social systems generate patterns that may be described, modeled, and interpreted, but they cannot be fully apprehended from any single vantage point. Structural analysis clarifies tendencies and boundary conditions; it does not produce definitive judgments about particular institutions, actors, or events.

Within the framework of Occupational Psychosis, analytic claims are confined to structural dynamics and theoretical boundary models. This volume does not establish empirical thresholds, predictive probabilities, diagnostic criteria, or evaluative instruments. It does not determine whether any specific institution exhibits distortion, nor does it authorize external adjudication.

The purpose of this chapter is to define the limits of inference that properly accompany institutional analysis. Analysis must remain proportionate to evidence.

Limits of Structural Inference

Structural sociology emphasizes patterned tendencies rather than individualized assessment (Merton, 1968; March & Olsen, 1989). Systems theory recognizes that observation is always situated within a perspective (Luhmann, 1995). Organizational analysis identifies bounded rationality and interpretive mediation as inherent features of decision environments (Simon, 1947; Weick, 1995).

Under such conditions, analytic models describe structural possibility rather than empirical certainty. Drift dynamics, convergence conditions, and reflexive constraints represent conceptual constructs designed to clarify how distortion may become stabilized, not to determine when it has occurred.

Institutional systems are dynamic, multi-layered, and context dependent. Observable variance may reflect adaptation rather than drift. Stability may reflect resilience rather than closure. Apparent convergence may reflect consensus rather than attenuation. Structural analysis cannot substitute for contextual judgment.

The Problem of Overreach

The articulation of theoretical boundary conditions carries risk of interpretive overreach. Concepts describing reflexive constraint or structural convergence may be mistakenly applied as diagnostic labels. Complex institutional phenomena may be reduced to simplified narratives of failure, capture, or collapse.

Within Occupational Psychosis, such overreach exceeds analytic intent. The framework does not authorize classification of institutions as "psychotic," dysfunctional, corrupt, or irredeemable. It does not designate sectors, professions, or governance forms as inherently prone to distortion.

The term "psychosis," as clarified earlier in this volume, functions as an analogical descriptor of structural reality distortion under specific compounded conditions. It does not imply clinical diagnosis, psychological pathology, or moral indictment. Analytic restraint is essential to prevent conceptual misapplication.

Contextual Variability

Institutional environments differ in size, mandate, complexity, stakeholder plurality, and governance architecture. Drift dynamics may manifest differently across contexts. In some environments, feedback loops remain robust; in others, reflexive pacing may vary. External accountability may be structured differently across jurisdictions.

Because institutional structures vary, analytic generalizations must remain conditional. No single dynamic, pattern, or boundary condition is sufficient to determine systemic distortion. Nor does the absence of such dynamics guarantee reflexive integrity. Institutional analysis identifies structural tensions, not definitive conclusions.

The Limits of Detection

Chapters 27 through 30 describe perception constraints, correction mediation, accountability boundaries, and rare structural closure conditions. These constructs illuminate how detection may be limited by structural architecture. They do not establish detection criteria, authorize scoring mechanisms, define thresholds of impossibility, or generate institutional verdicts. Epistemic humility requires acknowledging that institutional systems cannot be exhaustively evaluated from abstract models alone.

Separation from Governance and Reform

This volume does not prescribe governance redesign, policy intervention, regulatory reform, leadership strategy, or corrective programming. It neither recommends nor rejects specific reform approaches.

Governance design, stewardship architecture, and applied corrective frameworks require distinct analytic foundations and normative commitments. Those considerations exceed the descriptive and theoretical scope of this volume.

Volume II remains analytic. Application belongs to separately governed structures.

Boundary Clarification

The framework of Occupational Psychosis is conceptual and architectural. It clarifies how role-induced distortion may emerge and stabilize under compounded structural conditions. It does not claim universal applicability, predictive authority, or evaluative jurisdiction.

Any attempt to transform these analytic constructs into diagnostic tools, compliance frameworks, certification instruments, or sector-specific critiques exceeds the scope of this volume and ethics. Institutional analysis must remain proportionate, conditional, and structurally grounded.

If structural drift dynamics clarify how distortion may emerge, and structural impossibility defines a theoretical outer limit, then the final task is to define what this volume does not do, how it differs from governance and reform frameworks, and under what conditions responsible application may occur.

The concluding section therefore establishes explicit analytic boundaries. It distinguishes this volume from governance authority, reform advocacy, and certification mechanisms. It clarifies the conditions under which the concepts presented here may be responsibly interpreted without exceeding their epistemic limits.

Having established the epistemic boundary of institutional analysis, the remaining task is to clarify the scope and limits of this volume itself. The concluding section therefore delineates what this analysis does not do, how it differs from governance and reform frameworks, and the conditions under which its use remains conceptually appropriate.

ANALYTIC BOUNDARIES

CHAPTER 32

WHAT THIS VOLUME DOES NOT DO

This volume defines and analyzes structural dynamics associated with role-induced distortion within institutional systems. It articulates conceptual models, boundary conditions, and analytic constraints. It does not extend beyond that scope.

Delimitation of scope strengthens analytic integrity by preventing conceptual overreach and preserving methodological discipline. Clarifying what this volume does not do is therefore not a retreat from its claims, but a reinforcement of its structural precision. The purpose of this chapter is to clarify the negative perimeter of Volume II, what the analysis does not claim, authorize, or establish.

It Does Not Diagnose Institutions

This volume does not diagnose individual institutions, professions, sectors, or governance bodies. It does not classify organizations as distorted, dysfunctional, or structurally impaired. It does not determine whether Occupational Psychosis is present in any particular institutional context.

The constructs presented in this volume describe structural possibility under compounded dynamics. They do not function as criteria for classification or adjudication. Institutional analysis is descriptive, not declarative.

It Does Not Establish Measurement Instruments

Although structural dynamics are described with conceptual clarity, this volume does not provide measurement tools, scoring systems, detection protocols, assessment frameworks, or evaluative instruments. It does not define thresholds of distortion, specify indicators of severity, or offer comparative benchmarks. The analytic architecture outlined in this volume is non-instrumental.

It Does Not Prescribe Reform

This volume does not recommend governance redesign, policy intervention, leadership strategy, regulatory reform, professional restructuring, or corrective programming.

The distinction between analysis and prescription is deliberate. Structural explanation does not imply normative instruction. Reform, where appropriate, requires separate frameworks grounded in applied governance theory, ethical deliberation, and institutional context. Volume II remains analytic rather than programmatic.

It Does Not Target Sectors or Professions

The structural dynamics described in this volume are not limited to any specific sector, profession, or institutional form. Nor are they uniquely attributable to particular domains of authority.

This volume does not identify industries, public bodies, nonprofit organizations, entrepreneurial ecosystems, academic institutions, religious organizations, or professional fields as inherently prone to distortion. The analytic model applies to institutional architecture as such, not to named entities. Application to particular contexts requires disciplined contextual inquiry beyond the scope of this volume.

It Does Not Pathologize Individuals

The term "Occupational Psychosis" functions as an analogical descriptor of structural distortion under compounded conditions. It does not imply clinical diagnosis, psychological disorder, or individual pathology. No claim is made regarding the mental health, competence, character, or moral integrity of institutional actors. Structural analysis does not substitute for psychological assessment or ethical judgment. Role-induced distortion, as conceptualized here, operates at the level of system architecture rather than individual psyche.

It Does Not Predict Collapse

This volume does not assert that institutions inevitably drift toward closure, entrenchment, or breakdown. The boundary models described in Part V clarify structural limits under rare convergence conditions; they do not predict trajectory or frequency. Institutions regularly adapt, recalibrate, and renew. Structural mediation does not negate adaptive capacity. Analytic articulation of possibility does not constitute prediction of outcome.

It Does Not Confer Authority

This volume does not grant authority to readers to evaluate, label, audit, certify, or publicly adjudicate institutions using the constructs described herein.

Institutional analysis requires contextual evidence, disciplined methodology, and clearly defined governance authority. The framework presented in Volume II does not independently authorize such activity. Interpretation without appropriate structural, methodological, and governance grounding exceeds the scope of this text.

Methodological Position

The analytic posture adopted in this volume reflects traditions within structural sociology, institutional theory, and systems analysis (Merton, 1968; March & Olsen, 1989; Luhmann, 1995). These traditions emphasize patterned dynamics and boundary conditions rather than individualized attribution. The purpose of this volume is to clarify structural architecture, not to produce institutional verdicts.

If Volume II does not diagnose, measure, prescribe, target, pathologize, predict, or confer authority, then a further distinction is required: how analytic description differs from governance design and reform frameworks.

The following chapter clarifies that distinction explicitly. It separates structural analysis from stewardship authority and reform implementation, ensuring that analytic clarity is not mistaken for governance mandate.

CHAPTER 33

DISTINCTION FROM GOVERNANCE AND REFORM

Institutional analysis and institutional governance are distinct domains of inquiry. Structural description does not inherently confer authority to prescribe corrective action, redesign systems, or implement reform. Volume II operates within the domain of analytic clarification. It identifies structural dynamics, interpretive constraints, and boundary conditions under which role-induced distortion may emerge and stabilize. It does not establish governance mandates or reform pathways. The distinction between analytic architecture and governance authority is deliberate.

Analysis Is Not Administration

Structural sociology and institutional theory traditionally separate explanation from administration (Merton, 1968; March & Olsen, 1989). Descriptive models illuminate patterned dynamics; governance design involves normative commitments, value judgments, risk tolerances, and contextual decision-making.

Governance requires specification of objectives, accountability structures, stakeholder priorities, and implementation constraints. These decisions extend beyond analytic mapping. They require institutional legitimacy and authorized decision processes. Volume II does not engage in those processes.

Reform Requires Normative Commitment

Reform is not purely structural. It reflects normative choices about what constitutes improvement, stability, equity, efficiency, or legitimacy. Institutional redesign involves trade-offs across competing values and constituencies.

The structural dynamics described in this volume do not prescribe which trade-offs should be made, nor do they privilege particular governance philosophies. They describe possible constraints on perception and correction; they do not dictate institutional redesign. The absence of prescription is methodological discipline, not analytic omission.

Governance Authority and Jurisdiction

Governance authority operates within defined institutional mandates. Boards, executive bodies, regulatory agencies, professional associations, and legislative institutions hold specific jurisdictional authority to design, amend, and enforce structural change.

Analytic frameworks may inform governance deliberation, but they do not substitute for it. The translation from structural insight to institutional action requires formal authority, procedural legitimacy, and contextual knowledge. Volume II does not claim such authority.

The Risk of Conflation

When analytic models are conflated with reform mandates, two distortions may arise:

1. Structural description may be misinterpreted as evaluative verdict.

2. Conceptual frameworks may be prematurely operationalized without contextual grounding.

Both outcomes exceed the intended scope of this volume. Institutional stability depends upon preserving distinctions between observation, deliberation, and decision. Structural analysis clarifies observation; governance structures deliberate; authorized bodies decide. Maintaining these distinctions supports institutional coherence.

Stewardship and Application

Application of structural insights whether in governance design, corrective intervention, or institutional stewardship requires additional methodological, ethical, and jurisdictional frameworks.

Those frameworks must specify authority to act, scope of intervention, evidence standards, stakeholder engagement, and accountability structures. Such considerations extend beyond descriptive structural analysis. Volume II therefore remains intentionally non-programmatic.

Boundary Clarification

This chapter does not deny that structural analysis may inform governance deliberation. Nor does it suggest that reform is unnecessary or inadvisable. It clarifies that analytic description and governance action occupy different domains of responsibility.

Occupational Psychosis, as articulated in this volume, is an analytic construct. Governance, stewardship, and reform require distinct institutional mandates and applied frameworks. Conflation of these domains risks both analytic distortion and governance overreach.

If Volume II does not prescribe reform and does not confer governance authority, the final question concerns responsible interpretation. Under what conditions may structural analysis be engaged constructively without exceeding its scope?

The closing chapter articulates conditions for responsible application. It establishes interpretive discipline and safeguards against conceptual misuse, ensuring that analytic clarity remains proportionate to institutional responsibility. Distinction preserves integrity.

CHAPTER 34

CONDITIONS FOR RESPONSIBLE APPLICATION

Structural analysis carries interpretive consequences. Concepts describing institutional drift, reflexive constraint, and structural convergence can shape how institutions are understood and discussed. For this reason, the responsible engagement of analytic frameworks requires methodological discipline and proportional restraint.

Occupational Psychosis, as articulated in this volume, is a structural construct. It clarifies how role-induced distortion may emerge under compounded conditions. It does not authorize institutional labeling, public adjudication, or categorical classification. Responsible application begins with disciplined interpretation.

Condition One: Structural, Not Personal

Application of this framework must remain structural rather than individualized. Institutional distortion, as conceptualized here, operates at the level of architecture, feedback systems, authority loops, and interpretive stabilization.

Attributing distortion to individual intent, moral deficiency, or psychological pathology exceeds analytic scope. Structural dynamics may operate without malicious actors or conscious coordination. Responsible interpretation therefore avoids personalization.

Condition Two: Contextual Grounding

Institutional systems vary in mandate, scale, governance design, and environmental complexity. Structural dynamics described in this volume may manifest differently across contexts or may not manifest at all.

Application requires contextual grounding rather than abstract extrapolation. Isolated dynamics cannot be assumed to constitute compounded convergence. Partial observations do not establish structural closure. Responsible application remains conditional.

Condition Three: Non-Diagnostic Restraint

The framework presented in Volume II does not establish diagnostic criteria. It does not specify thresholds, severity scales, or determination protocols.

Responsible engagement therefore refrains from declaring institutions "distorted," "closed," or "structurally impossible to correct." Such determinations require contextual evidence, governance authority, and formal evaluative processes beyond the scope of this volume. Structural possibility does not equate to institutional verdict.

Condition Four: Governance Respect

Institutional reform and corrective intervention require authorized decision-making bodies. Governance design, policy revision, and structural redesign are legitimate functions of institutional leadership and oversight authorities.

Responsible application of this framework does not bypass governance channels or substitute analytic models for institutional mandate. Structural insight may inform deliberation, but it does not replace procedural legitimacy. Institutional coherence depends upon preserving this distinction.

Condition Five: Proportional Interpretation

Institutional systems are dynamic and adaptive. Drift dynamics, perception constraints, and convergence conditions may be counterbalanced by renewal mechanisms, leadership transitions, stakeholder pluralism, and environmental change.

Responsible interpretation therefore avoids absolutism. It recognizes contingency, variability, and institutional resilience. Structural analysis clarifies possibility, not inevitability.

Methodological Integrity

The conditions outlined above reflect longstanding traditions in structural sociology and institutional analysis (Merton, 1968; March & Olsen, 1989; Luhmann, 1995). These traditions emphasize patterned dynamics, contextual sensitivity, and limits of inference.

Analytic clarity depends upon maintaining proportionality between conceptual model and institutional complexity. Responsible application preserves that proportionality.

CONCLUSION: FROM FAILURE MODES TO INSTITUTIONAL RESPONSIBILITY

Occupational Psychosis was introduced as a conceptual lens through which structural distortion in institutional systems may be understood. Across this volume, structural preconditions, drift dynamics, detection limits, and epistemic boundaries have been clarified.

The purpose of this work is neither condemnation nor reform mandate. It is architectural illumination. Institutional systems are capable of resilience, adaptation, and renewal. Structural analysis does not diminish that capacity; it clarifies conditions under which reflexive integrity may require attention.

Where analysis ends, governance begins. Where structural possibility is identified, institutional responsibility remains with authorized bodies. The concepts articulated in this volume describe structural architecture under specific compounded conditions. They do not confer judgment, predict outcome, or determine institutional fate. Clarity requires restraint. Restraint preserves legitimacy.

This volume has defined *Occupational Psychosis* as a structural phenomenon emerging at the intersection of role identity, authority insulation, metric substitution, narrative stabilization, and reflexive constraint. It has articulated how such dynamics may accumulate gradually, how detection may be structurally mediated, and how analytic limits must govern interpretation.

What remains is not verdict but vigilance, structural awareness grounded in proportionality. Institutional systems endure not through perpetual suspicion, but through disciplined reflexivity. The aim of this work is to support that reflexivity without exceeding its mandate. Structural possibility, once understood, invites thoughtful governance, not reaction.

With this boundary established, Volume II concludes.

GLOSSARY OF STRUCTURAL TERMS

The following glossary defines key structural terms used throughout this volume. These definitions are conceptual and analytic in nature. They are provided to clarify terminology and maintain interpretive precision.

The terms below are not additive or cumulative; the presence or discussion of one construct does not imply the presence, severity, or determination of another. The entries below do not establish diagnostic criteria, evaluative thresholds, measurement constructs, or operational instruments. They are not intended for classification, assessment, institutional labeling, or procedural application. The terms describe structural dynamics as articulated within the analytic framework of this volume; they do not constitute standards of determination or institutional verdict.

Interpretation of these constructs should remain proportionate, contextual, and consistent with the analytic limits established in Chapters 32-34.

Core Structural Constructs

Authority Insulation

A structural condition in which decision-making authority becomes progressively buffered from corrective feedback through procedural layering, interpretive reinforcement, or hierarchical mediation. Authority insulation describes reduced permeability within governance architecture and does not imply intent, concealment, or misconduct.

Boundary Erosion

A gradual attenuation of institutional distinctions between roles, mandates, or procedural domains. Boundary erosion may occur through incremental reinterpretation or functional overlap and does not inherently signify institutional failure.

Compounded Convergence
The alignment of multiple structural dynamics in mutually reinforcing ways. Compounded convergence refers to the interaction of distinct drift patterns under sustained stabilization. It is theoretical and does not imply frequency or inevitability.

Diffusion of Responsibility
A distributional pattern in which decision accountability becomes dispersed across multiple actors or procedural layers. Diffusion describes structural allocation of responsibility rather than individual avoidance.

Drift Dynamics
Gradual shifts in institutional interpretation, procedural alignment, or structural emphasis that accumulate incrementally over time. Drift dynamics are characterized by stabilization rather than rupture and may occur within adaptive systems.

Epistemic Boundary
The limit of inference appropriate to a given analytic model. An epistemic boundary clarifies what may reasonably be concluded from structural observation and what exceeds disciplined interpretation.

External Accountability Constraint
A structural limitation arising from jurisdictional differentiation, translation mechanisms, or temporal pacing between institutional systems. External constraint refers to inter-system coordination limits rather than oversight deficiency.

Identity-Role Fusion
A structural alignment in which institutional identity becomes tightly integrated with role expectations or authority functions. Under certain compounded conditions, such fusion may reduce interpretive flexibility. It does not imply psychological pathology.

Incentive Alignment
The structural configuration of reward systems, recognition patterns, and performance expectations within institutional architecture. Incentive alignment describes coordination between institutional goals and operational metrics without presuming distortion.

Interpretive Convergence
The progressive narrowing of institutional meaning-making frameworks such that alternative interpretations become less visible within dominant narratives. Interpretive convergence may reflect coherence or stabilization and does not inherently denote dysfunction.

Metric Substitution
A structural shift in which quantitative indicators gradually function as proxies for institutional purpose or mission. Metric substitution refers to the elevation of measurable outputs within decision processes without implying intentional misrepresentation.

Moral Credentialing
A structural reinforcement dynamic in which institutional legitimacy narratives strengthen internal cohesion. Moral credentialing describes narrative stabilization mechanisms rather than moral deficiency.

Narrative Capture
A condition in which institutional interpretation becomes increasingly organized around dominant explanatory frames. Narrative capture describes interpretive stabilization rather than suppression or concealment.

Narrative Stabilization
The consolidation of institutional self-understanding through repeated framing and reinforcement. Narrative stabilization supports coherence and continuity but may, under certain compounded dynamics, reduce interpretive variance.

Professional Identity Lock-In
A structural condition in which institutional identity and professional norms become tightly interwoven with prevailing interpretive frameworks. Lock-in describes reduced adaptive bandwidth rather than individual rigidity.

Recursive Authority Loop
A reinforcing cycle in which authority decisions validate interpretive frameworks that, in turn, reaffirm authority structures. Recursive loops are structural features of institutional systems and may contribute to stability or reflexive constraint.

Reflexive Constraint
A reduction in institutional capacity to reexamine foundational assumptions. Reflexive constraint refers to mediated self-examination rather than incapacity or collapse.

Signal Attenuation
A structural filtering process through which variance information becomes moderated or reframed as it moves across hierarchical layers. Signal attenuation describes translation dynamics without implying distortion of intent.

Structural Closure
A rare theoretical boundary condition in which multiple reinforcing dynamics reduce the availability of corrective pathways within an existing institutional architecture. Structural closure is conceptual and does not establish permanence or inevitability.

Structural Constraint
A coordination or interpretive limitation emerging from institutional architecture. Structural constraint describes mediated responsiveness rather than failure or incapacity.

Structural Drift
Incremental divergence between institutional purpose and operational emphasis occurring without overt disruption. Structural drift is gradual and may remain within adaptive bounds.

Structural Possibility
The analytic recognition that certain institutional outcomes may arise under specific compounded dynamics. Structural possibility does not indicate probability, prediction, or institutional determination.

Structural Preconditions
Foundational institutional configurations that shape how authority, identity, incentives, and interpretation interact. Structural preconditions do not independently establish distortion.

System Differentiation
The structural separation of institutional domains such as governance, oversight, or operational functions into distinct decision logics. Differentiation supports complexity management and does not inherently create distortion.

Systemic Drift
A patterned shift across multiple institutional domains resulting from cumulative drift dynamics. Systemic drift is descriptive and non-diagnostic.

Temporal Misalignment
A structural divergence between pacing of internal recalibration and external review cycles. Temporal misalignment refers to coordination timing rather than oversight inadequacy.

Limits of Detection Terms

Correction Mediation
The structured process through which institutional systems recalibrate in response to variance. Mediation reflects procedural coordination rather than resistance.

Detection Constraint
Structural limits affecting how institutions perceive, interpret, or register variance. Detection constraint does not imply incapacity or inevitability.

Structural Impossibility (Theoretical Limit Condition)
A conceptual boundary model describing conditions under which corrective pathways may become functionally inaccessible within a given architecture. Structural impossibility is rare, theoretical, and non-predictive.

Analytic Boundary Terms

Analytic Construct

A conceptual model developed to describe patterned structural dynamics. An analytic construct does not function as a diagnostic instrument or evaluative authority.

Institutional Verdict

A categorical determination assigning evaluative status to an institution. The framework of this volume does not produce institutional verdicts.

Non-Instrumental Analysis

A form of structural inquiry that does not generate measurement tools, operational criteria, or prescriptive guidance.

Proportional Interpretation

The disciplined alignment of analytic claims with evidentiary limits and contextual variability.

The terms defined above are components of a structural analytic framework. They are not diagnostic categories, institutional classifications, or governance directives. Their purpose is conceptual clarification within the analytic scope established throughout this volume.

Structural terminology, when used proportionately and contextually, supports disciplined interpretation rather than institutional adjudication.

REFERENCES

Chapter 1

Argyris, C. (1991). Teaching smart people how to learn. *Harvard Business Review*, 69(3), 99–109.

DiMaggio, P. J., & Powell, W. W. (1983). The iron cage revisited: Institutional isomorphism and collective rationality in organizational fields. *American Sociological Review*, 48(2), 147–160.

Janis, I. L. (1982). *Groupthink: Psychological studies of policy decisions and fiascoes* (2nd ed.). Houghton Mifflin.

Merton, R. K. (1936). The unanticipated consequences of purposive social action. *American Sociological Review*, 1(6), 894–904.

Vaughan, D. (1996). *The Challenger launch decision: Risky technology, culture, and deviance at NASA*. University of Chicago Press.

Weber, M. (1978). *Economy and society* (G. Roth & C. Wittich, Eds.). University of California Press. (Original work published 1922)

Weick, K. E., & Sutcliffe, K. M. (2007). *Managing the unexpected: Resilient performance in an age of uncertainty* (2nd ed.). Jossey-Bass.

Chapter 2

Ashforth, B. E., & Mael, F. (1989). Social identity theory and the organization. *Academy of Management Review*, 14(1), 20–39.

Berger, P. L., & Luckmann, T. (1966). *The social construction of reality*. Anchor Books.

Freidson, E. (2001). *Professionalism: The third logic*. University of Chicago Press.

Gioia, D. A., Patvardhan, S. D., Hamilton, A. L., & Corley, K. G. (2013). Organizational identity formation and change. *Academy of Management Annals*, 7(1), 123–193.

Janis, I. L. (1982). *Groupthink: Psychological studies of policy decisions and fiascoes* (2nd ed.). Houghton Mifflin.

Schein, E. H. (2010). *Organizational culture and leadership* (4th ed.). Jossey-Bass.

Tajfel, H., & Turner, J. C. (1979). An integrative theory of intergroup conflict. In W. G. Austin & S. Worchel (Eds.), *The social psychology of intergroup relations* (pp. 33–47). Brooks/Cole.

Chapter 3

Argyris, C., & Schön, D. A. (1978). *Organizational learning: A theory of action perspective.* Addison-Wesley.

Foucault, M. (1977). *Discipline and punish: The birth of the prison.* Pantheon Books.

Janis, I. L. (1982). *Groupthink: Psychological studies of policy decisions and fiascoes* (2nd ed.). Houghton Mifflin.

Merton, R. K. (1968). Bureaucratic structure and personality. In *Social theory and social structure* (pp. 195–206). Free Press. (Original work published 1940)

Weber, M. (1978). *Economy and society* (G. Roth & C. Wittich, Eds.). University of California Press. (Original work published 1922)

Weick, K. E. (1995). *Sensemaking in organizations.* Sage.

Weick, K. E., & Sutcliffe, K. M. (2007). *Managing the unexpected: Resilient performance in an age of uncertainty* (2nd ed.). Jossey-Bass.

Chapter 4

Espeland, W. N., & Sauder, M. (2007). Rankings and reactivity: How public measures recreate social worlds. *American Journal of Sociology*, 113(1), 1–40.

Goodhart, C. A. E. (1975). Problems of monetary management: The U.K. experience. In *Papers in monetary economics* (Vol. 1, pp. 91–121). Reserve Bank of Australia.

Merton, R. K. (1968). Social theory and social structure. Free Press. (Original work published 1940; see discussion of unintended consequences and goal displacement.)

Muller, J. Z. (2018). *The tyranny of metrics*. Princeton University Press.

Power, M. (1997). *The audit society: Rituals of verification*. Oxford University Press.

Strathern, M. (1997). "Improving ratings": Audit in the British University system. *European Review*, 5(3), 305–321.

Weick, K. E. (1995). *Sensemaking in organizations*. Sage.

Chapter 5

DiMaggio, P. J., & Powell, W. W. (1983). The iron cage revisited: Institutional isomorphism and collective rationality in organizational fields. *American Sociological Review*, 48(2), 147 160.

Kerr, S. (1975). On the folly of rewarding A while hoping for B. *Academy of Management Journal*, 18(4), 769–783.

Merton, R. K. (1968). Social theory and social structure. Free Press. (Original discussion of goal displacement and unintended consequences.)

March, J. G., & Olsen, J. P. (1989). *Rediscovering institutions: The organizational basis of politics*. Free Press.

North, D. C. (1990). *Institutions, institutional change and economic performance*. Cambridge University Press.

Pfeffer, J., & Salancik, G. R. (1978). *The external control of organizations: A resource dependence perspective*. Harper & Row.

Selznick, P. (1957). *Leadership in administration*. Harper & Row.

Chapter 6

Berger, P. L., & Luckmann, T. (1966). *The social construction of reality*. Anchor Books.

DiMaggio, P. J., & Powell, W. W. (1983). The iron cage revisited: Institutional isomorphism and collective rationality in organizational fields. *American Sociological Review*, 48(2), 147–160.

Goffman, E. (1959). *The presentation of self in everyday life*. Anchor Books.

Meyer, J. W., & Rowan, B. (1977). Institutionalized organizations: Formal structure as myth and ceremony. *American Journal of Sociology*, 83(2), 340–363.

Selznick, P. (1957). *Leadership in administration*. Harper & Row.

Suchman, M. C. (1995). Managing legitimacy: Strategic and institutional approaches. *Academy of Management Review*, 20(3), 571–610.

Weick, K. E. (1995). *Sensemaking in organizations*. Sage.

Chapter 7

Argyris, C., & Schön, D. A. (1978). *Organizational learning: A theory of action perspective*. Addison-Wesley.

Berger, P. L., & Luckmann, T. (1966). *The social construction of reality*. Anchor Books.

Janis, I. L. (1982). *Groupthink: Psychological studies of policy decisions and fiascoes* (2nd ed.). Houghton Mifflin.

Kuhn, T. S. (1962). *The structure of scientific revolutions*. University of Chicago Press.

Merton, R. K. (1968). *Social theory and social structure*. Free Press.

Weick, K. E. (1995). *Sensemaking in organizations*. Sage.

Chapter 8

Argyris, C., & Schön, D. A. (1978). *Organizational learning: A theory of action perspective*. Addison-Wesley.

Hirschman, A. O. (1970). *Exit, voice, and loyalty*. Harvard University Press.

Janis, I. L. (1982). *Groupthink: Psychological studies of policy decisions and fiascoes* (2nd ed.). Houghton Mifflin.

Morrison, E. W., & Milliken, F. J. (2000). Organizational silence: A barrier to change and development in a pluralistic world. *Academy of Management Review*, 25(4), 706–725.

Weick, K. E. (1995). *Sensemaking in organizations*. Sage.

Chapter 9

Asch, S. E. (1955). Opinions and social pressure. *Scientific American*, 193(5), 31–35.

DiMaggio, P. J., & Powell, W. W. (1983). The iron cage revisited: Institutional isomorphism and collective rationality in organizational fields. *American Sociological Review*, 48(2), 147–160.

Kerr, S. (1975). On the folly of rewarding A while hoping for B. *Academy of Management Journal*, 18(4), 769–783.

March, J. G., & Olsen, J. P. (1989). *Rediscovering institutions: The organizational basis of politics*. Free Press.

Merton, R. K. (1968). *Social theory and social structure*. Free Press.

Morrison, E. W., & Milliken, F. J. (2000). Organizational silence: A barrier to change and development in a pluralistic world. *Academy of Management Review*, 25(4), 706–725.

Chapter 10

Meyer, J. W., & Rowan, B. (1977). Institutionalized organizations: Formal structure as myth and ceremony. *American Journal of Sociology*, 83(2), 340–363.

Power, M. (1997). *The audit society: Rituals of verification*. Oxford University Press.

Merton, R. K. (1968). *Social theory and social structure*. Free Press. (Discussion of ritualism and goal displacement.)

DiMaggio, P. J., & Powell, W. W. (1983). The iron cage revisited: Institutional isomorphism and collective rationality in organizational fields. *American Journal of Sociology*, 48(2), 147–160.

Selznick, P. (1957). *Leadership in administration*. Harper & Row.

Chapter 11

Weber, M. (1978). *Economy and society* (G. Roth & C. Wittich, Eds.). University of California Press.

Selznick, P. (1957). *Leadership in administration*. Harper & Row.

March, J. G., & Olsen, J. P. (1989). *Rediscovering institutions: The organizational basis of politics*. Free Press.

Michels, R. (1911/1962). *Political parties: A sociological study of the oligarchical tendencies of modern democracy*. Free Press.

DiMaggio, P. J., & Powell, W. W. (1983). The iron cage revisited: Institutional isomorphism and collective rationality in organizational fields. *American Journal of Sociology*, 48(2), 147–160.

Chapter 12

Ashforth, B. E., & Anand, V. (2003). The normalization of corruption in organizations. *Research in Organizational Behavior*, 25, 1–52.

Bandura, A. (1999). Moral disengagement in the perpetration of inhumanities. *Personality and Social Psychology Review*, 3(3), 193–209.

Meyer, J. W., & Rowan, B. (1977). Institutionalized organizations: Formal structure as myth and ceremony. *American Journal of Sociology*, 83(2), 340–363.

Selznick, P. (1957). *Leadership in administration*. Harper & Row.

Suchman, M. C. (1995). Managing legitimacy: Strategic and institutional approaches. *Academy of Management Review*, 20(3), 571–610.

Weber, M. (1978). *Economy and society*. University of California Press.

Chapter 13

Foucault, M. (1977). *Discipline and punish: The birth of the prison*. Pantheon. (Discussion of discourse and institutional power.)

Lakoff, G. (2004). *Don't think of an elephant! Know your values and frame the debate.*

Chelsea Green. (Framing and interpretive structure.)

Meyer, J. W., & Rowan, B. (1977). Institutionalized organizations: Formal structure as myth and ceremony. *American Journal of Sociology*, 83(2), 340–363.

Selznick, P. (1957). *Leadership in administration*. Harper & Row.

Suchman, M. C. (1995). Managing legitimacy: Strategic and institutional approaches. *Academy of Management Review*, 20(3), 571–610.

Weick, K. E. (1995). *Sensemaking in organizations*. Sage.

Chapter 14

Agamben, G. (2005). *State of exception*. University of Chicago Press. (Concept of prolonged exceptional framing; cited for theoretical grounding, not event commentary.)

Beck, U. (1992). *Risk society: Towards a new modernity*. Sage.

Merton, R. K. (1968). *Social theory and social structure*. Free Press. (Goal displacement and unintended consequences.)

March, J. G., & Olsen, J. P. (1989). *Rediscovering institutions: The organizational basis of politics*. Free Press.

Weick, K. E., & Sutcliffe, K. M. (2007). *Managing the unexpected: Resilient performance in an age of uncertainty*. Jossey-Bass.

Chapter 15

Abbott, A. (1988). *The system of professions: An essay on the division of expert labor*. University of Chicago Press.

March, J. G., & Olsen, J. P. (1989). *Rediscovering institutions: The organizational basis of politics*. Free Press.

Merton, R. K. (1968). *Social theory and social structure*. Free Press.

Selznick, P. (1957). *Leadership in administration*. Harper & Row.

Weber, M. (1978). *Economy and society*. University of California Press.

Chapter 16

Vaughan, D. (1996). *The Challenger launch decision: Risky technology, culture, and deviance at NASA*. University of Chicago Press.

Merton, R. K. (1968). *Social theory and social structure*. Free Press.

March, J. G. (1994). *A primer on decision making: How decisions happen*. Free Press.

Weick, K. E. (1995). *Sensemaking in organizations*. Sage.

Chapter 17

Darley, J. M., & Latané, B. (1968). Bystander intervention in emergencies: Diffusion of responsibility. *Journal of Personality and Social Psychology*, 8(4), 377–383.

March, J. G., & Olsen, J. P. (1989). *Rediscovering institutions: The organizational basis of politics*. Free Press.

Merton, R. K. (1968). *Social theory and social structure*. Free Press.

Weick, K. E. (1995). *Sensemaking in organizations*. Sage.

Vaughan, D. (1996). *The Challenger launch decision: Risky technology, culture, and deviance at NASA*. University of Chicago Press.

Chapter 18

Suchman, M. C. (1995). Managing legitimacy: Strategic and institutional approaches. *Academy of Review*, 20(3), 571–610.

Selznick, P. (1957). *Leadership in Management administration*. Harper & Row.

March, J. G., & Olsen, J. P. (1989). *Rediscovering institutions: The organizational basis of politics*. Free Press.

Rhee, M., & Valdez, M. E. (2009). Contextual factors surrounding reputation damage with potential implications for reputation repair. *Academy of Management Review*, 34(1), 146–168.

Weick, K. E. (1995). *Sensemaking in organizations*. Sage.

Chapter 19

Abbott, A. (1988). *The system of professions: An essay on the division of expert labor*. University of Chicago Press.

Freidson, E. (2001). *Professionalism: The third logic*. University of Chicago Press.

March, J. G., & Olsen, J. P. (1989). *Rediscovering institutions: The organizational basis of politics*. Free Press.

Merton, R. K. (1968). *Social theory and social structure*. Free Press.

Selznick, P. (1957). *Leadership in administration*. Harper & Row.

Chapter 20

Argyris, C., & Schön, D. A. (1978). *Organizational learning: A theory of action perspective*. Addison-Wesley.

March, J. G. (1994). *A primer on decision making: How decisions happen*. Free Press.

March, J. G., & Olsen, J. P. (1989). *Rediscovering institutions: The organizational basis of politics*. Free Press.

Weick, K. E. (1995). *Sensemaking in organizations*. Sage.

Luhmann, N. (1995). *Social systems*. Stanford University Press.

Chapter 21

Argyris, C., & Schön, D. A. (1978). *Organizational learning: A theory of action perspective*. Addison-Wesley.

March, J. G. (1994). *A primer on decision making: How decisions happen*. Free Press.

Weick, K. E. (1995). *Sensemaking in organizations*. Sage.

Luhmann, N. (1995). *Social systems*. Stanford University Press.

Vaughan, D. (1996). *The Challenger launch decision: Risky technology, culture, and deviance at NASA*. University of Chicago Press.

Chapter 22

March, J. G. (1994). *A primer on decision making: How decisions happen*. Free Press.

March, J. G., & Olsen, J. P. (1989). *Rediscovering institutions: The organizational basis of politics*. Free Press.

Selznick, P. (1957). *Leadership in administration*. Harper & Row.

Weick, K. E. (1995). *Sensemaking in organizations*. Sage.

Vaughan, D. (1996). *The Challenger launch decision: Risky technology, culture, and deviance at NASA*. University of Chicago Press.

Chapter 23

Weick, K. E. (1995). *Sensemaking in organizations*. Sage.

March, J. G., & Olsen, J. P. (1989). *Rediscovering institutions: The organizational basis of politics*. Free Press.

Selznick, P. (1957). *Leadership in administration*. Harper & Row.

Ricoeur, P. (1984). *Time and narrative* (Vol. 1). University of Chicago Press.

Luhmann, N. (1995). *Social systems*. Stanford University Press.

Chapter 24

March, J. G. (1994). *A primer on decision making: How decisions happen*. Free Press.

Meyer, J. W., & Rowan, B. (1977). Institutionalized organizations: Formal structure as myth and ceremony. *American Journal of Sociology*, 83(2), 340–363.

Power, M. (1997). *The audit society: Rituals of verification*. Oxford University Press.

Weick, K. E. (1995). *Sensemaking in organizations*. Sage.

Selznick, P. (1957). *Leadership in administration*. Harper & Row.

Chapter 25

Argyris, C., & Schön, D. A. (1978). *Organizational learning: A theory of action perspective*. Addison-Wesley.

Festinger, L. (1957). *A theory of cognitive dissonance*. Stanford University Press.

March, J. G., & Olsen, J. P. (1989). *Rediscovering institutions: The organizational basis of politics*. Free Press.

Weick, K. E. (1995). *Sensemaking in organizations*. Sage.

Luhmann, N. (1995). *Social systems*. Stanford University Press.

Chapter 26

Argyris, C., & Schön, D. A. (1978). *Organizational learning: A theory of action perspective*. Addison-Wesley.

DiMaggio, P. J., & Powell, W. W. (1983). The iron cage revisited: Institutional isomorphism and collective rationality in organizational fields. *American Sociological Review, 48*(2), 147–160.

March, J. G., & Olsen, J. P. (1976). Organizational choice under ambiguity. In

J. G. March & J. P. Olsen (Eds.), *Ambiguity and choice in organizations* (pp. 10–23). Universitetsforlaget.

Meyer, J. W., & Rowan, B. (1977). Institutionalized organizations: Formal structure as myth and ceremony. *American Journal of Sociology, 83*(2), 340–363.

Weick, K. E. (1995). *Sensemaking in organizations*. Sage Publications.

Weick, K. E., & Sutcliffe, K. M. (2007). *Managing the unexpected: Resilient performance in an age of uncertainty* (2nd ed.). Jossey-Bass.

Chapter 27

Argyris, C., & Schön, D. A. (1978). *Organizational learning: A theory of action perspective*. Addison-Wesley.

Luhmann, N. (1995). *Social systems*. Stanford University Press.

March, J. G. (1994). *A primer on decision making: How decisions happen*. Free Press.

March, J. G., & Olsen, J. P. (1989). *Rediscovering institutions: The organizational basis of politics*. Free Press.

Meyer, J. W., & Rowan, B. (1977). Institutionalized organizations: Formal structure as myth and ceremony. *American Journal of Sociology*, 83(2), 340–363.

Selznick, P. (1957). *Leadership in administration*. Harper & Row.

Simon, H. A. (1947). *Administrative behavior*. Macmillan.

Weick, K. E. (1995). *Sensemaking in organizations*. Sage.

Chapter 28

Argyris, C., & Schön, D. A. (1978). *Organizational learning: A theory of action perspective.* Addison-Wesley.

Luhmann, N. (1995). *Social systems.* Stanford University Press.

March, J. G. (1994). *A primer on decision making: How decisions happen.* Free Press.

March, J. G., & Olsen, J. P. (1989). *Rediscovering institutions: The organizational basis of politics.* Free Press.

Meyer, J. W., & Rowan, B. (1977). Institutionalized organizations: Formal structure as myth and ceremony. *American Journal of Sociology*, 83(2), 340–363.

Selznick, P. (1957). *Leadership in administration.* Harper & Row.

Weick, K. E. (1995). *Sensemaking in organizations.* Sage.

Chapter 29

Luhmann, N. (1995). *Social systems.* Stanford University Press.

March, J. G., & Olsen, J. P. (1989). *Rediscovering institutions: The organizational basis of politics.* Free Press.

Meyer, J. W., & Rowan, B. (1977). Institutionalized organizations: Formal structure as myth and ceremony. *American Journal of Sociology*, 83(2), 340–363.

Power, M. (1997). *The audit society: Rituals of verification.* Oxford University Press.

Selznick, P. (1957). *Leadership in administration.* Harper & Row.

Chapter 30

Argyris, C., & Schön, D. A. (1978). *Organizational learning: A theory of action perspective.* Addison-Wesley.

Luhmann, N. (1995). *Social systems*. Stanford University Press.

March, J. G. (1994). *A primer on decision making: How decisions happen*. Free Press.

March, J. G., & Olsen, J. P. (1989). *Rediscovering institutions: The organizational basis of politics*. Free Press.

Selznick, P. (1957). *Leadership in administration*. Harper & Row.

Weick, K. E. (1995). *Sensemaking in organizations*. Sage.

Chapter 31

Luhmann, N. (1995). *Social systems*. Stanford University Press.

March, J. G., & Olsen, J. P. (1989). *Rediscovering institutions: The organizational basis of politics*. Free Press.

Merton, R. K. (1968). *Social theory and social structure*. Free Press.

Simon, H. A. (1947). *Administrative behavior*. Macmillan.

Weick, K. E. (1995). *Sensemaking in organizations*. Sage.

Chapter 32

Luhmann, N. (1995). *Social systems*. Stanford University Press.

March, J. G., & Olsen, J. P. (1989). *Rediscovering institutions: The organizational basis of politics*. Free Press.

Merton, R. K. (1968). *Social theory and social structure*. Free Press.

Simon, H. A. (1947). *Administrative behavior*. Macmillan.

Chapter 33

Luhmann, N. (1995). *Social systems.* Stanford University Press.

March, J. G., & Olsen, J. P. (1989). *Rediscovering institutions: The organizational basis of politics.* Free Press.

Merton, R. K. (1968). *Social theory and social structure.* Free Press.

Selznick, P. (1957). *Leadership in administration.* Harper & Row.

Chapter 34

Luhmann, N. (1995). *Social systems.* Stanford University Press.

March, J. G., & Olsen, J. P. (1989). *Rediscovering institutions: The organizational basis of politics.* Free Press.

Merton, R. K. (1968). *Social theory and social structure.* Free Press.

Selznick, P. (1957). *Leadership in administration.* Harper & Row.

Simon, H. A. (1947). *Administrative behavior.* Macmillan.

CITATION GUIDANCE

Citation Guidance

This work is intended to be cited as a conceptual, diagnostic, and analytical text, not as a methods manual or applied intervention guide.

Occupational Psychosis (Volume I) establishes the originating definition of the concept. Subsequent volumes extend structural classification, institutional analysis, and governance considerations within the Occupational Wellness Institute Canon.

When referencing specific institutional failure modes, citations should include both the volume and chapter designation to preserve structural context and prevent interpretive fragmentation.

Use of the term *Occupational Psychosis* should maintain alignment with its defined conceptual scope and should not be generalized to describe individual pathology, workplace dissatisfaction, or isolated leadership behavior.

Recommended Citation (APA 7th Edition)

Arts, G. L. (2026). *Occupational psychosis: The hidden crisis beneath occupational wellness.* Occupational Wellness Institute.

Arts, G. L. (2026). *Occupational psychosis: Institutional failure modes.* Occupational Wellness Institute.

Arts, G. L. (2026). *Occupational psychosis: Authority, ethics, and governance.* Occupational Wellness Institute.

Notes for APA Users

- Capitalize only the first word of the title and subtitle, and proper nouns.
- Italicize the book title.
- Cite this work as conceptual, diagnostic, and analytical in nature.

Recommended Citation (Chicago Manual of Style, 17th Edition)

Notes and Bibliography Format

Arts, Georgia Lee. *Occupational Psychosis: The Hidden Crisis Beneath Occupational Wellness.* United States: Occupational Wellness Institute, 2026.

Arts, Georgia Lee. *Occupational Psychosis: Institutional Failure Modes.* United States: Occupational Wellness Institute, 2026.

Arts, Georgia Lee. *Occupational Psychosis: Authority, Ethics, and Governance.* United States: Occupational Wellness Institute, 2026.

Author-Date Format

Arts, Georgia Lee. 2026. *Occupational Psychosis: The Hidden Crisis Beneath Occupational Wellness.* United States: Occupational Wellness Institute.

Arts, Georgia Lee. 2026. *Occupational Psychosis: Institutional Failure Modes.* United States: Occupational Wellness Institute.

Arts, Georgia Lee. 2026. *Occupational Psychosis: Authority, Ethics, and Governance.* United States: Occupational Wellness Institute.

Notes for Chicago Users

- Use headline-style capitalization for the title and subtitle.
- Location may be omitted if not required by the journal or institution.
- Cite this work as a foundational diagnostic and analytical text.

Attribution Standard

References to the Occupational Wellness Institute Canon should preserve authorship, canonical structure, and conceptual integrity.

Attribution should include the author (Georgia Lee Arts) and the canonical title. Where applicable, inclusion of the volume designation is recommended to maintain structural context.

Canonical terminology should be cited as defined and should not be reclassified, paraphrased, or presented as an independent methodology, framework, or intervention model.

CANON INDEX

Occupational Wellness Institute Canon

Canon Designation Mark (CDM): 💎 – Verified Canonical Volume

The following index defines the structured body of work designated under the Occupational Wellness Institute Canon. Canonical volumes establish the formal analytic foundation of the field and are governed as an integrated intellectual system.

Canonical Classification Key
💎 Canonical Volume
P Public Access
R Restricted Access (Institutional / Controlled Distribution)

Arts, Georgia Lee

💎 **Occupational Psychosis: The Hidden Crisis Beneath Occupational Wellness (P)**
Designated canonical volume. Diagnostic and definitional in scope; non-operational.

💎 **Occupational Psychosis: Institutional Failure Modes, Volume II (P)**
Designated canonical volume. Structural classification of institutional distortion patterns; non-prescriptive.

💎 **Occupational Psychosis: Authority, Ethics, and Governance, Volume III (R)**
Designated canonical volume. Examination of governance constraints, ethical boundaries, and institutional authority dynamics.

Forthcoming Canonical Volumes

Additional volumes within the Occupational Wellness Institute Canon are in development and will extend the field across stewardship, institutional application, and advanced governance structures.

Detailed classification and access designation will be formally issued at the time of publication.

Pre-Canonical Works by the Author

The following works were published prior to the formal establishment of the Occupational Wellness Institute Canon.

Arts, Georgia Lee

The $2 Trillion Revenue Gap™: How Identity Misalignment Is Silently Costing America Trillions and How Identity Alignment Transforms People, Workplaces, and Communities
Applied analysis written for public, organizational, and policy audiences.

Dream Journey, Breaking the Dream Barriers™: A Guide to Bridging Identity Gaps in Life and Career
Conceptual and narrative work exploring identity, meaning, and personal inquiry.

ABOUT THE AUTHOR

Georgia Lee Arts is the founder and research architect of the Occupational Wellness Institute™. Her work focuses on occupational wellness, identity alignment, ethical governance, and the structural conditions that shape modern work, leadership, and institutional life.

With a background spanning military service, organizational leadership, human development, and scholarly inquiry, Arts brings a systems-level lens to questions often addressed only at the individual or symptomatic level. Her work examines how roles, incentives, authority structures, and professional architectures influence perception, judgment, ethics, and identity, frequently in ways that remain invisible within conventional wellness and leadership paradigms.

Arts' writing is characterized by a disciplined separation between definition, analysis, and application, emphasizing conceptual clarity, structural precision, and institutional responsibility. Her canonical work contributes to emerging discourse at the intersection of occupational psychology, organizational behavior, identity science, systems analysis, and governance.

She resides in the United States and continues to develop institutional research and canonical scholarship through the Occupational Wellness Institute™.

INDEX

adaptive language, 14, 159, 161

ambiguity, 95, 188, 229

analytic boundaries, 193

authority, vi, viii, vi, vii, ix, xi, xii, 18, 19, 20, 22, 23, 26, 27, 28, 29, 31, 33, 34, 37, 41, 46, 48, 51, 52, 56, 70, 71, 72, 73, 74, 75, 76, 77, 78, 79, 82, 83, 84, 85, 87, 90, 91, 92, 93, 94, 95, 96, 98, 103, 107, 108, 109, 110, 112, 113, 114, 118, 119, 120,121, 122, 124, 125, 126, 127, 128, 129, 130, 134, 135, 139, 144, 150, 156, 160, 161, 169, 171, 172, 174, 177, 184, 185, 193, 198, 199, 200, 201, 203, 204, 206, 207, 209, 210, 211, 214, 215, 216, 237, 239

compounding, 34, 36, 40, 45

conditional, 31, 34, 192, 193, 207

coordination constraints, 171, 175, 180

corrective feedback, 19, 20, 22, 34, 41, 45, 130, 143, 160, 210

cross-boundary detection, 180

detection constraint, 215

dissent, 20, 27, 28, 40, 58, 59, 60, 61, 63, 124, 127, 154, 158, 180

drift, 13, 21, 38, 40, 99, 104, 108, 115, 118, 127, 135, 139, 144, 150, 156, 191, 192, 208, 211, 214, 215

epistemic limits, 190, 193

escalation, 126

feedback suppression, 52, 55, 56, 60, 63, 98, 130

institutional distortion, 21, 206

interpretive, 14, 118, 125, 135, 139, 143, 154, 156, 158, 159, 165, 168, 174, 177, 184, 212

interpretive convergence without contestability, 153, 154

legitimacy, ix, 20, 23, 26, 31, 33, 36, 37, 42, 44, 46, 48, 52, 53, 60, 66, 67, 69, 70, 71, 74, 75, 76, 77, 78, 79, 81, 82, 85, 88, 93, 95, 97, 112, 113, 115, 117, 120, 122, 145, 152, 161, 169, 174, 175, 178, 179, 201, 202, 203, 207, 209, 212, 220, 223, 224, 225

manifestation, vii, 19, 22, 67, 71, 83, 135, 140, 145

metric, 13, 14, 35, 36, 38, 58, 63, 67, 73, 150, 152, 165, 168, 177, 212 metric stability amid outcome variance, 147, 148

narrative capture, 23, 42, 45, 46, 51, 71, 77, 79, 83, 85, 87, 90

narrative coherence, 18, 19, 22, 37, 44, 46, 58, 77, 84, 143, 146, 147

narrative over-integration, 143, 146, 150, 156

narrative over-integration, 14

narrative reinforcement, vii, xi, 18, 34, 48

non-crisis conditions, 138

normalization, 86, 87, 88, 89, 90, 91, 93, 94, 95, 98, 102, 104, 105, 134, 140, 223

occupational psychosis, vi, viii, vi, vii, x, xi, 18, 19, 20, 22, 25, 28, 31, 33, 36, 37, 40, 41, 45, 46, 51, 53, 56, 60, 62, 65, 67, 69, 71, 75, 77, 78, 80, 83, 85, 87, 90, 94, 97, 98, 102, 104, 107, 111, 113, 116, 117, 120, 124, 128, 133, 137, 138, 142, 143, 146, 148, 153, 154, 159, 167, 170, 171, 175, 176, 180, 183, 187, 190, 191, 193, 197, 199, 204, 206, 209, 234, 235, 237

operational, 31, 84

perception, xi, 22, 86, 112, 114, 167, 168, 169, 170, 174, 180, 183, 192, 203, 208, 239

recalibration, 35, 40, 41, 46, 72, 77, 78, 82, 84, 87, 89, 90, 91, 93, 95, 97, 102, 103, 104, 107, 108, 109, 110, 113, 114, 115, 116, 119, 125, 127, 138, 139, 140, 142, 144, 145, 146, 148, 150, 161, 169, 171, 172, 174, 178, 180, 183, 184, 185, 186, 215

recalibration delay under non-crisis conditions, 140

reflexive, ix, 18, 19, 21, 22, 26, 27, 28, 31, 32, 33, 40, 41, 46, 48, 51, 120, 184, 185, 187, 191, 192, 206, 209, 214

signal attenuation, 133, 134, 135, 136, 214

signal attenuation across hierarchical layers, 131

specialization, 18, 19, 27, 120, 169, 171

specialization,, 18, 19, 27, 120, 171

structural analysis, xi, xii, 200, 204

structural conditions, vi, vii, ix, xi, 18, 19, 20, 21, 23, 25, 28, 33, 34, 38, 47, 53, 60, 63, 69, 71, 72, 77, 78, 82, 84, 93, 95, 97, 112, 116, 117, 120, 124, 128, 129, 130, 137, 145, 146, 153, 159, 167, 170, 185, 193, 239

structural convergence, 191, 206

structural probabilities, vi, xii

structural reinforcement, 156, 174, 212

systemic, 99, 174, 215

temporal, 87, 90, 93, 95, 98, 104, 138, 139, 140, 142, 150, 153, 178, 179, 180, 211

www.ingramcontent.com/pod-product-compliance
Ingram Content Group UK Ltd.
Pitfield, Milton Keynes, MK11 3LW, UK
UKHW020841290926
15470UKWH00004B/1486

9 798994 127209